P9-DFD-787

Twayne's United States Authors Series

EDITOR OF THIS VOLUME
Kenneth E. Eble
*University of Utah,
Salt Lake City*

Frederick Manfred

TUSAS 336

Frederick Manfred

FREDERICK MANFRED

By ROBERT C. WRIGHT

Mankato State University

TWAYNE PUBLISHERS
A DIVISION OF G. K. HALL & CO., BOSTON

Published in 1979 by Twayne Publishers,
A Division of G. K. Hall & Co.
All Rights Reserved

Printed on permanent/durable acid-free paper and bound
in the United States of America

First Printing

Frontispiece photograph of Frederick Manfred
by Bruce Buursma.

Library of Congress Cataloging in Publication Data

Wright, Robert C
Frederick Manfred.

(Twayne's United States authors series : TUSAS 336)
Bibliography: p. 172 - 76
Includes index.
1.   Manfred, Frederick Feikema, 1912 -
—Criticism and interpretation.
PS3525.A52233Z95   813'.5'4   78-27676
ISBN 0-8057-7247-2

This Book is Dedicated
To My Wife,
Lorraine

Contents

About the Author

Robert C. Wright was born in Wayne, Nebraska, in 1921. He holds advanced degrees from the Universities of Texas and Nebraska, and he has had a year of post-doctoral study at the University of Washington. At present he is a Professor of English at Mankato State University, Mankato, Minnesota, where he served as departmental chairman between 1965 and 1975. He belongs to the honorary societies Sigma Tau Delta and Pi Delta Epsilon, having served on the Grand Council of the latter society for ten years, including a term as national president. He holds the Gold Key Award from the Columbia Scholastic Press Association. During World War II, he served in the Army Air Forces, where he was an associate editor for *Radar* magazine and on the staff of *Air Force*. His essay on Eugene O'Neill's *The Iceman Cometh* appeared in *Modern Drama* for May 1965. His essay entitled "The Myth of the Isolated Self in Manfred's Siouxland Novels" appears as a chapter in *Where the West Begins*, Center for Western Studies Press (Sioux Falls, S. D., 1978). He is presently engaged in research for a work on Minnesota writers and for a book on Frank Herbert.

Preface

This study has been designed to give the reader a complete overview of Frederick Manfred's work, including brief summaries of each book followed by comments which will identify themes and point up significant aspects. The commentaries are intended more as explicative criticism than as evaluative, as indicators of scholarly possibilities rather than as definitive statements on the books.

Titles are not arranged chronologically but rather according to categories which Manfred has found useful in discussing his work. The novels are primarily an interpretation of the farming experience in Siouxland; the tales have a base in historical events which happened during the nineteenth century in and around Siouxland; the rumes are basically autobiographical; the romances are complex explorations of personalities caught in contrasting rural and urban settings; and the stories and poems develop themes similar to those explored in the longer works. In Chapter Five, major themes are identified and traced through the works as a whole, and in the postscript, a brief evaluation is made of the Manfred career to date.

ROBERT C. WRIGHT

Mankato State University
Mankato, Minnesota

Acknowledgments

I wish to thank Frederick Manfred for his friendly cooperation during the writing of this book, especially for permission to read the manuscript 'copies of *Milk of Wolves* and *The Manly-Hearted Woman*.

The help of Alan Lathrop, Manuscripts Division, University of Minnesota Archives, is much appreciated.

For many hours of typing, I wish to thank Marge Tierney and my wife, Lorraine.

I appreciate the careful proofreading of Gloria Benson, and I am grateful to Russell Roth of *Modern Medicine* for reading and commenting on the manuscript.

I am indebted to Mankato State University for a Faculty Research Grant, Spring 1975.

Also acknowledged is permission to quote from other books copyrighted by Frederick Manfred and for permission to use material from unpublished manuscripts.

Finally, I wish to thank Leora Wright, my mother, who at ninety-two continues to be an inspiration through her courageous living.

Chronology

1912   January 6: Frederick Feikema born at Doon, Iowa.

1928   Graduated from Western Academy, a parochial high school in Hull, Iowa.

1929   April 19: death of mother, Alice (nee Van Engen).

1930   Entered Calvin College, Grand Rapids, Michigan.

1934   Graduated from Calvin College; returned to family farm near Doon, Iowa.

1934   Hitchhiked east and west, working at odd jobs.

1936   Moved to New Jersey. September: moved to Sioux Falls, South Dakota.

1937   Moved to Minneapolis to be sports reporter for the *Minneapolis Journal*.

1938   Helped organize American Newspaper Guild.

1939   January: left *Minneapolis Journal*.

1940   April: entered Glen Lake Tuberculosis Sanatorium, Oak Terrace, Minnesota. Met future wife, Maryanna Shorba.

1941   Published two essays, "In Defense of Women" and "Independence—Do We Lose It Under Stringent Laws?" in sanatorium magazine *Terrace Topics*.

1942   March: left Glen Lake Sanatorium. September: joined editorial staff of *Modern Medicine*, Minneapolis. October 31: married Maryanna Shorba, in Nashua, Iowa, in Little Church in the Wildwood.

1943   January: left *Modern Medicine*. Began full-time writing career in Minneapolis.

1944   Received Minnesota Regional Writing Fellowship. September: published *The Golden Bowl*. November 28: daughter Freya born.

1945   Awarded $1000 grant in aid from American Academy of Arts and Letters. April: moved to Bloomington, Minnesota. May: published short story, "Horse Touch," in *Northwest Life*. September: published short story, "Footsteps in the Alfalfa," in *Esquire*. November: published *Boy Almighty*.

1947   March: published *This is the Year*.

1948   April: published *The Chokecherry Tree*.

1949   Appointed writer in residence at Macalester College, St. Paul. Awarded a writing fellowship from the Andreas Foundation. Honored at the 1849 - 1949 Minnesota Territorial Centennial celebration as one of Minnesota's living greats. September: published *The Primitive*.

1950   September: published *The Brother*. December 5: daughter Marya born.

1951   January 28: presented a memorial address on the occasion of the burial of Sinclair Lewis' ashes. December: published *The Giant*.

1952   April 25: changed from pen name of Feike Feikema to Frederick Manfred.

1953   Published short story, "Where the Grass Grows Greenest," in two installments (June 6 and 20) in *The Farmer*.

1954   February 6: son Frederick born. September: published *Lord Grizzly*, first book in "Buckskin Man" series.

1956   September: published *Morning Red*.

1957   May: published *Riders of Judgment*, "Buckskin Man" series.

1959   June: published *Conquering Horse*, "Buckskin Man" series.

1960   September 1: moved to Luverne, Minnesota.

1961   October: published *Arrow of Love*, three novelettes.

1962   January: published *Wanderlust* trilogy, a revised version of *The Primitive*, *The Brother*, and *The Giant*.

1963   Awarded fellowship at Huntington Hartford Foundation.

1964   February: made thirteen half hour television tapes for KUSD-TV, University of South Dakota, entitled "Plainsong: Conversations with Frederick Manfred." November: published *Scarlet Plume*, "Buckskin Man" series.

1965   September: published *The Man Who Looked Like the Prince of Wales* (later entitled *The Secret Place*, published 1967).

1966   October: published *Winter Count* (poems).

1967   Awarded honorary life membership in Western Literature Association and presented with Distinguished Service Award.

1968   March: published *Apples of Paradise*, stories. September: published *Eden Prairie*. Appointed writer in residence at University of South Dakota, Vermillion.

1973   Nominated for fourth time for Nobel Prize for literature.
1974   Published *Conversations with Frederick Manfred,* moderated by John R. Milton, with a foreword by Wallace Stegner.
1976   Published *The Manly-Hearted Woman* and *Milk of Wolves.*
1977   Published *Green Earth.*

CHAPTER 1

Becoming a Prairie Watchman

I *Parentage and Early Years*

F REDERICK Manfred is a novelist dedicated to finding a "usable past" and to taking a "long view." He relies heavily in his writing upon his own heritage, which is half Frisian and half Saxon; but at the same time he carries a strong sense of what it means to be "American." In *Conversations With Frederick Manfred*, he says to John Milton, "It was great for me to learn that I was first of all not only an American as my grandfather and father always tried to tell me, but that I also had a lot of Old English blood in me."[1]

The Saxon line comes through his mother's family, the Van Engens. Frederick Van Engen, his maternal grandfather, was born June 6, 1861, in Coevorden, The Netherlands, and his great-grandfather, Harm Van Engen, was born in Emlichheim, Lower Saxony, Germany. In a trip to The Netherlands in the spring of 1974, Manfred was able to establish the roots of his mother's family tree.

The Frisian line comes from the Feikemas, whose home town was Tzum, near Franeker, West Friesland. Part of the original Friesland is now one of the eleven provinces in the nation known as The Netherlands. The four political divisions of Greater Friesland are Central Friesland in The Netherlands; and East Friesland, North Friesland, and Helgoland in Germany.[2] Frederick's paternal grandfather was Feike Feikes Feikema V, but when he came through Ellis Island, the customs officer suggested that he take the name of Frank, after the town. Before settling down, Frank tried several locations in the Midwest: Orange City, Iowa; Grand Rapids, Michigan; Perkins, Iowa; Lebanon, Missouri; The Badlands, South Dakota; and Doon, Iowa, where he worked as a stone mason. When his wife died, the family broke up. Both Manfred's father and his

15

Aunt Kathryn grew up with people of New England descent in Doon.

Manfred's parents, Frank Feikema (Feike Feikes Feikema VI) and Aaltje (Alice) Van Engen, farmed the rich gray loess found around Doon in northwest Iowa. Frederick Feikema was born January 6, 1912, the eldest of six brothers, all of whom are over six feet two inches tall. Many relatives called him Feike (Fy' kah), and he had it as a nickname through school days. But his mother called him Frederick, rarely Fred or Feike. When it was time to publish his first book, his publisher suggested the pen name Feike Feikema (Fy'kah Fy' kah-ma), though at the time he preferred a more American name. After his seventh book, he took that American name—Frederick Manfred.[3]

Of the Feikema brothers, Fred is tallest at six foot nine. His brothers are Edward, who makes cement well curbs in Doon; Floyd, an executive with a mortgage firm in Minneapolis; John, a mechanic and filling station owner in California; Abben, a navy man and mechanic; and Henry, a lawyer in the Twin Cities.

An accurate account of life in this largely male household is given in *Green Earth* and in Manfred's narrative poem "Winter Count," which covers the years from his birth to his mother's death when he was seventeen. A less autobiographical account of his youthful years on the farm is to be found in his novel *This is the Year*. Although it is not a "rume" and therefore not historically accurate, it nevertheless does give a true feeling for Manfred's early life. Such scenes as the harvesting episodes, the account of the grasshopper invasion, the strike, and the routine of farm chores are all rendered with the vividness of firsthand knowledge. Furthermore, specific events are often taken from actual experiences, such as Pier's fall from the windmill, which is an accurate description of a fall his father took. Neither Pier of the novel nor Frank Feikema learned to read, and Nertha died young as Alice Feikema did.

As a key to understanding the novelist, *This Is The Year* is especially important for the way it explains his Frisian heritage and dramatizes the problems associated with Americanization. Pier's father, Âlde Romke, represents the "old country" view of life, while Pier tries to forget old ways and language in an attempt to create an American identity. Ironically, in his own personality, Pier exemplifies the Frisian national traits. According to Dr. Bernard Fridsma, head of the Frisian Information Bureau, Frisians have always been known for independence, individualism, and a streak of stubbornness.[4] It is Pier's stubbornness that eventually causes him to lose his farm. Âlde Romke's pride in his Frisian-Holstein cattle, and Manfred's frequent reference to them in his books, are indications of national pride, for Frisian cattle have been and still are the base of the Frisian economy.

There is a Frisian saying that "the Frisian is never on the side of the majority." Their land has been traditionally a refuge for persecuted minorities, from Huguenots to Anabaptists and Labadists and Mennonites. Manfred confesses that as a youth he had a strong sense of belonging to a minority. "You've got one strike against you as a clodhopper," Manfred says. "Then in addition, I was a Frisian (C8). The Frisians were a minority group among the Hollanders, who were a minority within the American society. Manfred was set apart, too, by his height. At twelve, when he started high school, he was as tall as some of the seniors. "I was kind of a weird sight," he remembers. "I was slender, thin, awkward. Had big feet and hands, with little or no muscles. Just bones. . . . I suppose I was a misfit in some ways" (C8). He remembers not liking to have his picture taken, seeing the camera as an intrusion on his identity. He sees himself defending his territory much as a good dog would, tending to bark at people who invade his area. This kinship to canine ways is given full expression in one of his most recent books, *Milk of Wolves*, where he explores the relationship of the "outsider" to society. In explaining how his style differs from that of Sinclair Lewis, he has written, "He [Lewis] belonged to the cat family of writers and I to the bear. (He liked cats for pets and I liked dogs.)"[5] As an eldest son, he early had a strong sense of being alone and apart, with nothing around to play with but a dog and a teddy bear. "The dog and I ran off a couple of times together. Once he suggested it and once I did"(C18). Manfred's sense of aloneness may explain why he chose to make the hero of his rume *Wanderlust* an orphan, for intellectually as a youth he did feel orphaned.

However, he was not all that much alone. He had his mother and his Aunt Kathryn to learn from. His mother "didn't have a line of guile in her," he remembers. She was very warm, had musical talent, and spent much time playing rhyming games with her son. That musical talent she passed along to Manfred, who discovered it later in life and gave it also to Thurs Wraldson, hero of *Wanderlust*.

His Aunt Kathryn, sister to his father, was a tall woman "inclined to the beauties of life and not the crudities of life," Manfred recalls.

"How she managed to exist for some seventy years without really discovering she is a human animal is beyond me. . . . She is almost pure spirit" (C18). Some of these characteristics of Aunt Kathryn are given to Elizabeth in *Morning Red* and to Karen in *Eden Prairie*, where Manfred's country school experience is used to advantage. His Aunt Kathryn lived with the Feikemas when she was teaching in the home school, where young Fred was one of her pupils. In the poem "Winter Count," he tells of letting a mouse go in the school room while Kathryn was playing the organ. She screamed and jumped up on the stool. Kathryn was not resentful, but recognized the need to keep Fred's mind occupied; so she put him in two grades at once, first and second.

Kathryn also recognized early that Fred might be a writer, and, being author of a slim green volume of poetry, she encouraged him. Even before he started school, she was teaching him. She has told him of the time she interrupted her tatting to say, "Freddie, I don't know what's going to become of you. What are you going to become?"

"What's the hardest thing to become?" he asked.

"Become a poet," she said.

"Well, that's what I am going to be," the five year old replied (C19).

But Aunt Kathryn could not altogether make up for the lack of intellectual atmosphere surrounding Frederick during those early years. There were few books around, and his father could not read or write, though he was good at figures. However, there was the Bible. Because his mother wanted a man to read the Bible at family worship, the chore fell to Fred as oldest boy. He read the Dutch Bible first, then the English Bible, which he read through seven times before going to college. That reading has been important to the novelist, not only for the many allusions he is able to draw from it, such as in *Lord Grizzly*, but also for the way his phrases often carry a biblical rhythm and beauty.

Along with the daily Bible reading, Manfred's religious training was as a baptized member of the Christian Reformed Church, a denomination formed in 1857 in a split from the Reformed Church in America. It was a Calvinistic rearing in which the Bible was taken as infallible. The church ran a high school at Hull, Iowa, which Manfred attended as Western Academy. It is now Western Christian High School. During these years he put muscle on his bones and became an excellent baseball pitcher. He trained by running the seven and a half miles between his farm home and Hull.

Father, mother, and Aunt Kathryn were the important figures in Manfred's early life. Through the two women he learned sensitivity to aesthetic values, and through his father the "manly sweetness of life," the joy in physical labor and in play. He says his mother had a tremendous influence on him, but that his father had the most influence in the long run. "Which I thank God for. It's wrong when a son lets his mother put the final stamp on him (C24)." He saw his father as an old style hero. "When there was something to be done, he did it" (C61). Now Manfred thinks that his father probably had dyslexia, which might account for his inability to read. His father's second and third wives read to him, and thus he was able to know something of his son's creative talent.

II *College and Wanderlust*

Although Manfred wrote poems and love letters in high school, since he always had a girl in his life to serve as an ideal or "white goddess," he did not write seriously until he came at eighteen to Calvin College in Grand Rapids, Michigan. It, too, was supported by the Christian Reformed Church.

With his mother's death and his father's remarriage, he found himself free to go to college, provided he worked his way through. The working and the learning are quite accurately recorded in "The Primitive," first volume of the trilogy *Wanderlust*, a rume. It follows closely the events of his college years. Manfred's own literary bent is traded for musical talent in "The Primitive," whose hero, Thurs Wraldson, physically resembles Manfred. The events of his own life are all there: the dating, the playing of basketball, the debating, the learning.

One event, rather traumatic at the time, was his flunking of freshman English, but he has since seen that as an advantage. It let him know that he had to be different. "Something goes wrong in that critical atmosphere of the classroom which discourages the tiny little bud of writing," he thinks (C22). In fact, the most exciting learning experiences he got at Calvin were not in the classroom but in the Plato Club, run by Dr. Harry Jellema, his philosophy professor. As he describes it, the club was run like an informal graduate seminar, often meeting in homes. Members were elected into the group, and each night a student's paper was read and discussed. The discussion would often go on all night, with Dr. Jellema there as guide. The Plato Club served as a model for his own later teaching at Macalester College in St. Paul and at the University of South Dakota. The classrooms and the clubs of Calvin produced some other well-known writers: David Cornel De Jong, a novelist; Meindert De Jong, a writer of children's books; and Peter DeVries, a satiric novelist and humorist. All were rebels on the campus, Manfred says.

The rebellion, by and large, was against the fundamentalist position of the Christian Reformed Church, which up to this time had formed the base for Manfred's religious training. In "The Primitive," Thurs reflects Manfred's thinking as he prepares to write a paper on "Proofs of the Existence of God" for the Calvin College president. He finds no proofs in reading such writers as St. Augustine, Erasmus, Luther, Calvin, Aquinas. He saw all their elaborate guesses as based on the premise that the Bible was the literal word of God. Looking at it from the other side of the premise, Thurs saw the Bible in a new light, as a human document, a poetic history of a people, showing both the good and the bad aspects of an ambivalent world.[6] Also, in the informal "bull" sessions of the "brain trust," Thurs and his friends criticized the Christian religion for being dogmatic, for demanding absolute obedience and unquestioning faith in a world that is too complicated for easy either/or answers.[7]

If the intellectual climate at Calvin caused Manfred to question some of his earlier training and separated him from his home folks, on the other hand, being away also caused him to appreciate his upbringing on the farm and provided the emotional punch that pushed him into writing. "The first good thing I wrote was 'A Harvest Scene.' It was written on a day when I shot lonesome for home in memory." The piece described a day when he had been called home from a neighbor's to harvest one hundred and twenty acres of ripe grain for his father, who was ill with undulant fever. "I did it all alone. . . . My brothers brought a change of horses for me, but I just cut night and day until I had all of it cut. Before a storm. I never forgot the beauty of that on-coming storm" (C24). He wrote down his impressions of that day, not for class, but his philosophy professor liked it so well he suggested that the college paper publish it. Later a number of sketches and poems were published in *The Chimes*, the campus paper, and in *Prism*, the campus magazine.

These small successes in college did not mean much when he graduated in the midst of the Depression. He had a teaching certificate, but "wanderlust" was upon him and he took to the road.

Much as Thurs hitchhiked after college to find a job in the East, Manfred from 1934 to 1937 hitchhiked both east and west, working at odd jobs, but also writing sketches and reading widely. Following graduation from Calvin, he returned to the Iowa farm, but he soon left on a hitchhiking trip to Yellowstone National Park. His experiences on this trip were used later in his first novel, *The Golden Bowl*. However, he claims Maury Grant of that novel is not himself but rather is based on a cynical young man he met along the way. His subsequent trips east to Michigan and New Jersey were the basis for "The Brother," the second volume of the trilogy *Wanderlust*. He worked one winter in a warehouse in Michigan, and then he headed for the New York area, where he took a factory job with U. S. Rubber in Passaic, New Jersey. Although the novelist says his own life was somewhat different from and worse than the life he gave Thurs, many of his own experiences with the routine of factory work, with unions and with political bosses are reported in "The Brother." He reports also his introduction to Greenwich Village life and to the urban artistic community. He was in the New York area two different times: March to July in 1935 and January through March in 1936. On both occasions, he visited his Aunt Gertrude in Washington, D. C. and spent several weeks in that city.

Manfred became something of a hero in the Dutch district of Passaic, where he lived in 1936, because of his basketball ability and his work putting out a weekly called *The Prospector*, for which he wrote a column. He was encouraged to run for office as a Democrat, even though there was little chance he could win where there were nine Republicans to one Democrat. It was thought he might cut the ratio to two to one and help the Democrats win the state, thus giving Mayor Frank Hague that much more power. Manfred first asked to meet Mayor Hague, whom he describes as a "powerful man who scared the crap out of me in some ways." There was a short meeting at which Manfred asked: "Suppose I win? Am I free to vote my conscience?" The mayor couldn't believe what he was hearing; "You win," he scoffed, "and you've got to ask me for permission to piss."[8]

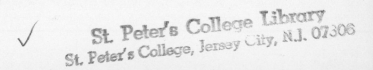

Many of these political experiences in New Jersey are used by
Manfred in *Morning Red,* where they are associated with events
supposedly happening in the Minneapolis - St. Paul area. Of his so-
journ in the East, he says he never seemed to feel rooted in and just
naturally started drifting west.

After his eight months in the New York area, he tried for work in
Washington, D. C., and then headed back to the farm. But he was
still restless and took to the road again, this time for California.
Soon he was back again in the Midwest. He tried to sell Jewel Tea
Company products in September and October of 1936 throughout
eastern South Dakota, then started working in the Sioux Falls
stockyards as an insurance investigator for the Hartford Insurance
Company, at eleven dollars a week. He lived in Sioux Falls from
September 1936 to March 1937 and played basketball for an in-
dependent team. In January he enrolled in Nettleton Commercial
College. As a basketball player for the Commercial College team he
remembers scoring fifty-seven points in one game. Many of his
Sioux Falls experiences as well as his high school years at Hull,
Iowa, were used in *The Chokecherry Tree.* Although Elof Lofblom
in that book is not Manfred, but is based on a friend of his who
visited him on the farm, he does claim to be "having a little sar-
donic play" with himself. "Many of the things that happened to
Elof happened to me in the summer of 1936." (C57)

I had been on the bum two years, as my dad says, out of college, and still I
hadn't made anything of myself. I came home actually without a pair of
shoes. In the book I have it that when Elof jumps out of the truck his shoes
fall to pieces. Well, that summer I wore rubbers, outdoor barnyard rubbers,
because we couldn't find shoes to fit me and I didn't have the money to
buy them. I was that broke (C57).

III   *Near Death and New Life in the Twin Cities*

Following his three months at Nettleton Commercial College,
Manfred took a job in Minneapolis as sports reporter for the old
Minneapolis Journal, where he helped organize the American
Newspaper Guild. During his two years with that paper, he again
was active in the labor movement and, as representative for the
guild, attended CIO meetings. Both Manfred and a fellow journalist, Eric Sevareid, were dropped from the *Journal* about the same
time, possibly because of their critical attitudes about the status

quo. Manfred had worked in his spare time for the reelection of Elmer Benson as governor. Manfred admits that he really wasn't a very good reporter. When he got interested in a story, he would spend too much time on it and would write too much. On other stories he wouldn't do enough. "I was good when I had to be and when I liked what I was looking at," he says.

He preferred following his own leads and writing his own material, especially after discovering at a party in 1937 that he could tell a tale his own way and make people listen. That was the night he found "his voice," or, as he now puts it, "his tone." He had dropped in late at a friend's party, a gathering of social workers and university people, and in response to a question about the South Dakota dust bowl in 1934, he started telling of his hitchhiking adventures. The people in the room turned toward him to listen, and he realized that he was telling the tale in a way that came naturally to him. After the party he went to his room and wrote that same tale all night, some fifty pages, and on into Sunday. He had found his own tone, or his own style, and had started what turned out to be his first published novel, *The Golden Bowl.*

During 1939 and 1940, after he left the *Journal,* Manfred worked hard to produce a publishable manuscript, so hard that he damaged his health by working long hours, smoking heavily, and eating improper food. "I practically lived on tapioca and coffee for a month," he says. "I think it helped me put a little realism in the passages describing hunger in my South Dakota characters." Furthermore, he was depressed over the rejection of his manuscripts, and as a consequence of his poor health, a tuberculosis germ laid him low. He thinks now he may have been exposed to TB when he lived in Sioux Falls. Critically ill, he was taken to Glen Lake Sanatorium in Oak Terrace, Minnesota, and very nearly died before passing the crisis and making a recovery.

The experience with tuberculosis provided material for his second novel, *Boy Almighty,* which he says is his most autobiographical work, with at least two-thirds of it taken directly from life. When he started writing the book, however, Eric Frey was modeled after the author's roommate, Howard Anderson, who was a fighter, agitating for this or that change in the sanitorium regimen and giving the nurses a bad time. Manfred thought this fighting spirit would pull Howard through, but it was the more passive novelist who survived. When the Howard material thinned out after forty pages or so, Manfred began to borrow heavily from his own experience. Writing the book was a way of forcing himself to remember a bad time that subconsciously he wanted to forget. He remembers thinking, "A callus or a veil or something was growing across my brain and shutting that whole experience out, and I didn't know whether I wanted that or not."

There were some good things to remember as well, for one of the patients at the sanatorium was a lovely girl named Maryanna Shorba, whom Manfred married on October 31, 1942. Maryanna had majored in journalism and minored in English at the University of Minnesota, where her classmates included such personalities as Max Shulman, Tom Heggen, and Norman Katkov. Over the years she has been an important sounding board for her husband and has become well known in Minnesota for her active support of the arts and humanities. Manfred says, however, that after the first book she never read any of his books in manuscript. Manfred was determined that there was to be but one tone in his books, his own.

Having struggled two years for their health in the sanatorium, the young couple after marriage had the courage and faith in themselves to give up regular employment in 1943 so that Manfred could begin a full-time career writing fiction. Following his illness, he had been employed briefly on the staff of the magazine *Modern Medicine*, but he had not as yet had a book published. Maryanna worked awhile for the *East Side Argus*, and Manfred helped. He also helped his new friend, Hubert H. Humphrey, who was running for mayor of Minneapolis. Serving as Humphrey's assistant campaign manager, Manfred came to respect that politician's integrity and his intellect. The possibility of a career in politics for himself was tempting to Manfred, who had strong feelings for the up and coming Democratic-Farmer-Labor Party in Minnesota. Humphrey wanted the novelist to stay with him even though he lost that initial campaign; but, aware of the political facts of life, the six foot nine Manfred said, "I am too big. When we step off a plane together everybody will look at me first, not you." Besides, Manfred said, he wanted to write novels.[9]

With the publication of *The Golden Bowl* in September of 1944, it looked as if he would have that chance. Response to the book was so favorable that he received a Minnesota Regional Writing Fellowship and attracted the attention of Sinclair Lewis, who was then living in Duluth and working on *Kingsblood Royal*. Frederick and Maryanna were invited to spend a long weekend with Lewis in Duluth, where he advised the younger writer to change publishers and to "Work, work, work. And it'll all bend before you."[10] Lewis had read *This Is The Year* in manuscript and used his influence to get it placed with Doubleday, with permission to quote his approval.

The midforties were good years for the couple. Their first child was born November 28, 1944, a daughter they named Freya (Frisian and Norse goddess of love and beauty); and they moved in 1945 to Wrâlda in Bloomington, where they bought ten acres on a bluff overlooking the Minnesota River valley. Manfred's books began coming off the presses at the rate of about one a year: *Boy Almighty* in 1945, *This Is The Year* in 1947, *The Chokecherry Tree* in 1948, and *The Primitive* in 1949. "Work, work, work," Sinclair Lewis had told him, and work he did. His five days a week routine was as follows: up at 6:30, breakfast alone while listening to music; work from 7:30 to noon; lunch on greens, skim milk, and cheese; correct copy until 3:00; walk for an hour; then read papers and have supper; read the masters in the evening.

That final year of the decade was a high point for the novelist. He accepted an appointment as "writer in residence" at Macalester College in St. Paul, received a writing fellowship from the Andreas Foundation, and was named one of Minnesota's living great, an award given as a part of the Minnesota Territorial Centennial celebration.

Those years in the Twin Cities provided much material for *The Giant*, final book in the trilogy, and for *Morning Red*. However, *The Giant* is the least autobiographical of the books in the trilogy. Manfred explains that Eva, the wife of Thurs, has in her a hint of his mother as well as of a woman named Professor Lucie Lawson, and is not a representation of his wife. However, the setting, the social structure described, the events, and many characters have a basis in fact from his early years in Minneapolis and St. Paul. The Bloomington property appears as the Thurs Wraldson estate overlooking the valley.

The estate also appears in *Morning Red*, where the Bloomington community is used as a setting for some scenes. Manfred took an interest in community affairs while he lived there, at one point stirring up a controversy when he launched a campaign to have a comprehensive zoning ordinance passed. When Manfred moved there, Bloomington was a town of about a thousand people, but it eventually did grow to the size of his invented city of Paineville. His Brokenhoe of *Morning Red* is located about where Savage is, and the corrupt political atmosphere of those suburbs is based in part on the historical events associated with Shakopee and Savage. The big storm and tornado he describes did occur in the Twin Cities, and newspaper accounts report many of the events he uses in *Morning Red*.

The promising career set in motion by his early novels and by the support of Sinclair Lewis seemed less assured as the three books in his trilogy came out in successive years: 1949, 1950, and 1951. The Eastern critics were not impressed with the "raw" exuberance of the midwesterner who dared find fault with the New York style of life. They did not like the liberties he took with language nor the way he mingled the comic with the serious. Manfred says he let Doubleday have his manuscripts for the trilogy before they were polished and had expected his publisher would also print the final version. They never did, but Alan Swallow encouraged him and published the one volume *Wanderlust* in 1962.

The early fifties were difficult for the novelist, who was trying to support his young family by his writing. Up to 1952 he never made more than $3000 a year. A second daughter, Marya, was born on December 5, 1950. The next month, while still recovering from an attack of flu, Manfred responded to a request to give the memorial address at the funeral of Sinclair Lewis in Sauk Center. In his remarks he referred to Lewis as his "friendly literary uncle—yes, even my father. . . . He showed me how he gathered his notes, how he organized them, how he executed them. He warned me about the various pitfalls that lay ahead for me; in particular telling me how I should handle that seemingly necessary evil—the critics."[11] In the eulogy, he recalled that the first Lewis book he read was *Elmer Gantry* and that the reading helped him in his determination not to become a minister, as his mother wished. His general assessment of the Lewis talent was that it illustrated "how an emotional force and mental brilliance lifted and developed an ordinary talent into greatness."[12] At the cemetery, in twenty-two below zero weather, Manfred observed a plume of steam arise from the urn when Lewis' ashes were poured over books in the grave. Manfred was overheard to say, "They tried to bring Red home, but at the last minute there he still got away." Later in *Riders of Judgment* he was to describe a similar phenomenon when Cain Hammett's coffin was opened.

When *The Giant* came out, in December of 1951, the critics continued their attack, and Manfred made two important decisions in an effort to get his reputation reestablished: he changed his pen name from Feike Feikema to Frederick Manfred, and he concentrated his creative energy on the story of mountain man Hugh Glass, a project he had been collecting material for since 1944. In desperate financial staits, he borrowed money and explained to his creditors how important his new novel was to his career, and they held his bills while he continued his research in South Dakota and finally published *Lord Grizzly* in September 1954. When it became a best seller and received critical acclaim, the crisis was over. As a good omen, in February of that year a son, Frederick, was born to the Manfreds. Encouraged by the success of *Lord Grizzly*, Manfred turned with confidence to the writing of the other novels which would become the Buckskin Man Tales. The late fifties, like the late forties, became years of high productivity, with a book coming out each year.

IV   *Siouxland and Blue Mound*

Dissatisfied with the ever-expanding city surrounding him, Manfred in 1960 moved to Luverne, Minnesota, at the heart of the area he had christened "Siouxland."[13] Luverne is on the Big Rock River in the southwestern corner of Minnesota, some twenty miles south of Pipestone, location of the sacred quarry in the Pipestone National Monument from which the Sioux Indians made their ceremonial pipes. Much of the action in *Scarlet Plume* and *Manly-Hearted Woman* centers in the Luverne area. The opening and closing scenes of *Milk of Wolves* are set in the Big Rock River valley, across which Manfred could look from his study perched atop Blue Mound. The Blue Mounds, made up of Sioux quartzite, rise three hundred feet above the Big Rock valley two miles north of Luverne. Lichen growing over the red rock gives the mounds a bluish green tinge as seen from a distance. Appropriately, Manfred chose a building site just under the brow of the southernmost outcropping, protected from the north wind and facing south toward his birthplace near Doon, Iowa, twenty-plus miles south just off Highway 75. Thus he now lives almost equidistant from the geographical centers most important to his career—the Indian culture symbolized in the pipestone quarry and the farming culture of his youth in Lyon County, Iowa, the Leonhard County in his books.

On Blue Mound Manfred built a home that not only matched his size but also gave him a link to nature and to the "old ones" he feels akin to as he writes. The back wall of the house is solid rock, and just a few steps from his study a remarkable row of rocks is lined up perfectly straight east and west (with the Equinox), put there he believes by prehistoric people to measure time. The buffalo jump described in *Scarlet Plume* is a short hike over the mound, and the amphitheater described in *Morning Red*, where Liz and Bert picnic and discover their love, is a feature of the area.

The building itself is one hundred and ten feet long, with its roof supported by three-by-twelve, rough cut red pine beams. The living room includes a kivalike conversation pit around a natural stone coffee table. The author's study, hexagonal in shape, is the only feature of the house that can be seen from the road below. It is connected to the living area below by a spiral staircase cut through the rock. During the building of the stairwell, Manfred fell through it and was seriously injured. The stairwell problem was only one of many Manfred encountered in building his unusual house. Transporting materials to the top of the mound was not easy, and costs rose to double the original estimates. He settled with the contractor out of court.

Because the Manfred property adjoined Blue Mounds State Park, the state recently purchased it and his house, which is now used as an Interpretative Center for the park. In August of 1975 Manfred moved from Blue Mound, and as of this writing he is living in the den-utility room of a new home being constructed on another high hill just across the valley. His "writing shack" is already in place and functioning. It is a small turquoise frame structure resembling a chicken coop, originally used on his Bloomington property.

Since 1968 Manfred has been "writer in residence" at the University of South Dakota in Vermillion. He makes the two hour drive every Monday during the school year to teach classes in creative writing.

During the 1975 - 1976 fall quarter he had his son Frederick in class, a senior majoring in communications, with good prospects for a career in television. The Manfred's eldest daughter, Freya, is a publishing poet who has participated in the "poetry in the schools program" in South Dakota and Massachusetts. During the 1975 - 1976 year she was a "fellow" at Radcliffe, where she was a "poet in residence." Marya, the second daughter, has been working in art, music, and poetry.

At the close of *Milk of Wolves*, Manfred has Juhl return to his home valley and, in walking to the source of the river, reflect on his life thus far. He is content with how he has lived it, just as Manfred is content. In *Conversations,* he says to John Milton: "I try to live each day complete, and to live it in such a way that I won't regret 'yesterday.' I can really say today, that I regret nothing that has ever happened to me. It's all fine with me." Milton then says, "And you've used most of it." Manfred replies, "What I have used, I have used, but I haven't begun to tap it yet."

Visitors to Manfred's Blue Mound home frequently were startled when they knocked on his door to have him appear above them on the peak of the roof, a human lightning rod silhouetted against the blue sky. This image forms an appropriate symbol of Manfred as a vertical mark on the horizontal prairie. He is a giant rod of a man, attracting to him the energy of the region from storms of human emotion and conflict. Through the magic of his art, the violent energies are passed to us safely and constructively as usable history and myth. He has become an ecclesiastical prairie watchman, fulfilling Kurt's dream in *Morning Red,* telling us that "the morning comes and also the night."

CHAPTER 2

Cultivating the Siouxland
Garden: Novels

I   The Golden Bowl (1944)

IN something of a mystical experience, Manfred one evening realized both that he was a "storyteller" and that he had had experiences worth telling. He wrote his first novel, *The Golden Bowl*, in a burst of creative energy following a Saturday night party at which he had entertained friends by telling them some of his hitchhiking adventures. After the party he went home, began writing, and continued working on the novel right through Sunday. Even though he felt exhilarated with this first effort, he says he later rewrote the book seven times—once as a play.[1]

Several of these drafts had been written when Steinbeck's *Grapes of Wrath* came out in 1940 with a dust bowl theme. The success of Steinbeck's novel encouraged Manfred to continue writing about his own country and in his own "voice." It is significant that in this first novel Manfred established not only a voice, but an attitude toward nature and the land that he would follow consistently through more than twenty novels. Nature is not, he believes, a malignant, malevolent force to be conquered, but rather it is a benign treasure to be accepted and protected.

In the course of *The Golden Bowl*, young Maury Grant learns this lesson. At the outset, he is a wandering victim of the Oklahoma dust bowl in 1934. He is bitter toward the land, but agrees to be a son to the Thor family in South Dakota. They need help in their battle against dust, but Maury wants to seek gold in the Black Hills. He stays with them only long enough to save the baby pigs, get a crop started, dig a well, and get the farmer's daughter, Kirsten, pregnant. Then he looks for work in the mines and in Montana, but he is overcome with loneliness and returns to the Thor family in time to help them weather another bad dust storm. After the storm, Pa Thor is still optimistic, and Maury does not mock him as he once did.

By referring to *Ecclesiastes* in choosing *The Golden Bowl*[2] as the title for his first book, Manfred calls attention to a tension of universal significance between man's desire to pull up roots and be free and his desire for rootedness and security. The writer of *Ecclesiastes* knows that the end of all pleasure is "dust," but he also reminds us that the wise man will stifle foolish hopes and try to accept conditions as they exist; it is foolish for man to suppose that he can escape his limitations.

The dust permeates the book, so much so that one reviewer complained of not being able to see the pages clearly. Certainly, Maury's personal struggle against the dust in the final episode is vividly portrayed, but it is the minor theme Manfred is playing. More significant is the implication that the very earth itself is dying, turning to dust as might an old man: "Slowly the drouth wrinkles the skin of the old creature. The veins, the hidden rivers, and once-swelling springs, dry up. The subsoil becomes brittle, and crumbles, and caves in. The topsoil crumbles, too, and collapses. And crevasses open the body"[3]. Early in the book, Manfred had described the result of spring rain on the land: "And vein roots swelled. New sprouts came. And the land, suddenly and incongruously, resembled an old man's face covered with a young man's fuzz" (11).

In such identification of man with earth, Manfred stresses the oneness of the universe. He sets up other natural symbols to represent the tension between "going" and "staying." When Pa Thor first meets Maury, the boy is singing the tumbleweed song, which identifies him as a wanderer. The tumbleweed is frequently associated with Maury; even in the final dust storm he feels the weed bump him and tumble on by.

The Thor family represents the stayers, the settled, those attached to the land who know their place. They quietly try to persuade Maury to stay with them, and their success can be measured in his several false starts. At one point Maury uses a little story to let Kirsten know he knows he is being pressured.

"Well, I was tired one day an' I lay down in the grass, an' I saw a thin green worm crawlin' on the end of a blade of grass. I watched it, reachin' an' lookin' an' reachin' fer some place to go. It reached, an' finally . . . I pushed another blade of grass so the worm could reach it. Then it crawled down an' hid in the deep roots."

Kirsten rubbed her legs, looking at him wonderingly.

"Sometimes I gotta feelin' that you people are pushing a blade a grass fer me." (99)

However, at this point Maury is not yet ready to "hide in the roots." The old life is too much with him. "No. I couldn't do it. Couldn't live here. I can't forget how my Pa an' Ma suffered. I don't wanna see it again. A man shouldn't have a brain, shouldn't have a memory . . . a memory is an awful thing" (99).

Before Maury can accept new parents and make a new home on the land, he must erase the sadness of the past from his memory in a rebirth from the womb of his earth mother. Such a symbolical experience is provided for him in the well digging episode, where he is lowered into the earth, is encased in water, and is pulled forth after being cramped into a fetal position. The episode also reveals a shift in power from Pa to Maury. When Ol' Gust wants to drink on the job, Maury says, "not here. Not while you're on the job for me." Ol' Gust is surprised and turns to Pa Thor, asking, "He the big shot here now?" (122). Maury is a young Telemachus visited by Athene and assuming command of the household of his father, Odysseus. Both Maury and Telemachus are searching for fathers.

When Maury complains about the horror of memory, he is taking the "short view," but his experience in the well and his later contemplation of the dinosaurs in the South Dakota Badlands initiate him into a new manhood and a "long view." That view is similar to the knowledge that comes to Pueblo Indian boys who spend eighteen months in a kiva after reaching twelve years of age. They enter the womb of mother earth, absorb the intuitive truth of the spirit, and emerge as men who, now freed from their mothers, are mature members of their tribe.

After Maury's experience in the well, he leaves for the Black Hills, Wyoming, and Montana, where he does not find work but does find the need to be "a unit of a tribe." He shares food with the lonely hoboes and admires their willingness to share what little they have, but in the end it is their separateness that he cannot abide.

Having been given the "long view," Maury on the way home realizes that he had been wrong. "He had for four years doubted the land. In the years to come, he would work doubly hard to make the earth, and his own heart, forget that he had been unfaithful" (196). Thus Maury, the pessimistic wanderer of the first chapter, through personal experience and mystical intuition, has become an optimistic member of a family, who foresees a schoolhouse full of his children and, in the midst of the black blizzard, can say of the house, "If it blows down, we'll build another (221)".

At that point, which is the end of the book, Maury doesn't know if the house will blow down or not. For the moment at least there is calm. He says, "I've been thinkin' that maybe we're in the middle of a cyclone" (224). The reader, too, is left in the eye of the storm. In an interview for *Critique,* Manfred explains that he realized that he stopped his book in the eye of a cyclone, that it was good because his spirit soared. "To me it's perfect," Manfred said. "I wouldn't want anything else. That symbol came up out of the country."[4]

For a first novel, *The Golden Bowl* was very well received by critics. In the *New York Times* (10/8/44), Andrea Parke calls the book a "timeless account of man's battle against nature and the gains measured only in the integrity of his own soul." A reviewer for the Autumn 1945 *Sewanee Review* sees it as a kind of folk ballad, "another lyric performance, a dexterous biography of the elemental forces which threaten the pioneer." Donald Bebeau, in the *South Dakota Review* (vol. 7, no. 4), believes Manfred's pruning "stops short of barrenness" and establishes a style of "simple dignity; earthy, rich in localisms." Wendell Johnson, on the other hand, in the *Chicago Sun Book Week* (9/10/44), thought that the story might be too big for the small canvas and that some incidents lacked motivation. Peter De Boer in his thesis on Manfred thought Maury's thoughts were too sophisticated for his character.[5] In spite of such reservations, the book picked up a following, largely for reasons such as those expressed by a reviewer for London's *The Listener* (5/27/48): "This is a comfortable and beautiful novel, achieving unpretentious perfection in its little field, and I'd prefer it to half a dozen howling Wolfes or straining Steinbecks."

II   This is the Year *(1947)*

Having written the autobiographical *Boy Almighty,* Manfred now chose to write about his home country, northwest Iowa, Siouxland. However, Pier Frixen in *This is the Year* is a contrast to Pa Thor of *The Golden Bowl,* for Pier does not love the land. There is a great temptation to read *This is the Year* as pure autobiography, with Pier as Manfred's father, but this reading would be a mistake, even though there are strong parallels to Manfred's life and times.

Now that the more truly autobiographical *Green Earth* has been published, the "fictions" in *This is the Year* can be readily seen.

Another temptation is to compare *This is the Year* to O. E. Rolvaag's *Giants in the Earth,* since both are set in Siouxland and have strong references to the immigrant adventure. Manfred remembers reading *Giants in the Earth* as a youth and thinking that Per Hansa's wagon could have crossed his land, that his very farm might, too, someday be a worthy subject to write about. *This is the Year* is the book he wrote, but it is not an updated *Giants,* even though both Pier and Per are lusty, energetic, and pugnacious, while their wives are brooding, timorous, and dissatisfied.

The novel covers the years 1918 to 1936, during which time Pier Frixen gains a wife and a farm, mistreats both, and loses all. The setting is northwestern Iowa, where Pier marries Nertha and rudely pushes his Frisian parents off the family farm. His first year's harvest is good, and a son is born, but Pier is worried. Success seems too easy. During the next six years Pier barely stays even with the land, which seems barren; and his wife is warned that she cannot have more children. Pier will not take the advice of his friendly county agent about conservation measures to save his farm. As a result, he is frequently in trouble with the unfriendly Peter Puddicomb, Blacktail as he is called, the deputy sheriff and implement dealer.

Pier, who never learned to read, sees some hope in his son, a bright boy who has a way with machines. Pier competes with his wife for influence over the boy, but Teo rejects both parents and hates farm work. Then parallel disasters hit farm and family: grasshoppers and dust storms strike, Nertha has a miscarriage, and Pier's father is killed while sawing wood. Pier is as outraged with the doctor who tells him Nertha's problems are his own fault as he is with the county agent who tells him his land is barren because he has failed to care for it.

Pier fights government men who want to vaccinate his cows, fights fellow farmers who are protesting low prices with a blockade, fights with his son, who has grown beyond him. When Nertha dies in another miscarriage, Pier feels guilty and thinks of suicide. But he marries Kaia, a gypsy widow who tricks him by pretending pregnancy. Pier throws her out, Teo leaves for college, Blacktail forecloses on the farm, and Pier heads out alone, saying to himself, "My heart's still green."

Weather and the soil are controlling influences in *This is the*

Year, performing somewhat the same function that the gods do in Greek literature, but also establishing the basic form and metaphor of the novel. Yet, while man's struggle with the elements provides the skeletal conflict, it is his struggle to understand himself in relationship to other human beings that shapes the flesh of the story and establishes the minor themes of social criticism and historical perspective. As Manfred put it in *Conversations*, the weather was the warp of the book and the people the woof (C86).

A. *Weather and Soil*

In an interview for *Critique*, Manfred explains that two versions of *This is the Year* were destroyed before the proper plot came to him while he was studying weather bureau records for the years 1918 through 1936. "I noticed five interestingly different swings in weather cycles and I thought, why not use this interesting weaving of the ups and downs. . . . They happened to fit the most dramatic years that I remember my uncles and my father living." He describes his basic concept as "the flowing seasons over the soil, rolling on almost like a cycle again."[6] There are five books, and each book has four parts representing the four seasons.

Pier Frixen and his fellow farmers are at the mercy of the weather, which, like some capricious Greek deity, gives and takes away crops. Frustrated, farmers talk endlessly about the weather and chafe at their inability to do anything about it. Always, though, they feel that "this is the year" for the bumper crop. Teo objects to missing school for farm work, and Pier rebuffs him:

"I'm sorry, boy. But I need you." Pier rubbed his chin. "Boy, this year, this year we gotta do it or we're done."

"You always say that. Every spring. And every spring I get sucked in by that fairy tale."

Pier growled. "Well, it isn't my fault, is it? I can't shake rain out a the sky, kin I?"[7]

Pier may not be able to do anything about the weather, but he can do something about the soil—only he will not. Nor will he make any effort to understand his wife, to "cultivate" her friendship and "fertilize" their relationship. This parallel between earth and woman is the controlling metaphor of the novel, a metaphor almost too persistently drawn. It is supported by Manfred's choice of "Nertha" as a name for Pier's wife. He explains that the Angles had a goddess of plenty, of cornucopia, named Nertha or Nerthus (C88).

Very early in the book the parallel is stated with grammatical emphasis: "It was spring and time to seed. It was time to cut his furrow on the land with a plow. It was time to cut his name on the stone of the future with a son" (10).

Pier visualizes the land as feminine: "He loved the land. The prairie seas, the sloping surfaces, caught his masculine eye. The vast earth was a wonderful giant of a woman. Her massive curves stirred the timeless bull in him" (21). He hopes Nertha will not grow to hate the land as Ma Lysbeth did, but Blacktail has predicted that hatred: "You and your Frisian-Holstein bulls. Too much in a hurry," he tells Pier on his wedding day. When Pier plows the land, he hurries in straight lines, refusing to take time to follow the contours; when he loves his wife, he hurries, thinking only of his own satisfaction. "The man and the plow and the horses were one, were the same, a bull; the earth a heifer beneath. . . . Relentlessly the plowing bull pursued the reeling heifer-earth. Soft and yielding, her soft fleshes ripped open, bleeding, running trickles of water, she suffered him his satisfaction" (130 - 31). Pederson, the county agent, knows how the land and a woman should be treated. He tries to warn Pier about his destruction of both: "Treat a woman right and she'll treat you right. Meal. Love. But treat her wrong, beat her, kick her, tear her clothes off, and she'll either whore or suicide" (316). This, of course, is what happens. Pier's land washes or blows away and will not bear crops; Nertha, in ironic contrast to her name, has two miscarriages and dies. The doctor tells Pier that Nertha's trouble is his fault for not giving her consideration and satisfaction; Pederson, the land doctor, blames him similarly for not treating his soil in a loving way. "You yourself sowed the seed of the rod that's now beating you, Pier," Pederson tells him at the final auction (603).

B.   *Human Relationships*

Pier wouldn't listen to Pederson in the role of land doctor, nor would he accept conversion when Pederson assumed the role of preacher, urging salvation through conservation. Manfred points out that preaching soil conservation, as such, was not Pederson's function so much as representing a new voice coming on—a voice Pier wouldn't listen to, not because he didn't have the brains, but because the "culture wasn't old enough yet to tell him how to use his talent."[8]

Another generation was needed, Teo's and Manfred's generation, before the Americanization process would be complete. Peter De Boer has identified Manfred's view as one of accepting the serviceable part of the past and rejecting that which retards—of accepting scientific knowledge in man's behalf, but rejecting destructive science.[9] Whether knowledge comes from the past or present, the important thing, according to Manfred, is to use it, but only after critical examination of its potential for good or bad.

Living almost totally in the present, Pier has trouble relating to the past, as represented in his parents, and to the future, as represented in Pederson, the Ol' Dreamer. "I don't care to remember," he tells his father (265). When the parents object to his marrying a girl who is part Norwegian, Pier flies into a rage: "Oh, fer godsakes, you an' yer damned nonsense about the Old Country. . . . Grow up. We're in Free America now. . . . An' talk American. I'm getting tired of that Old Country lingo" (33). Âlde Romke prophesies disaster for Pier and voices a refrain Pier himself will use at the end of the story: "Son, I deman' respect." He got none from Pier. Nor did Ma Lysbeth, who says to Pier, "Soan, you've got a heart as cold as ice an' as hard as stone" (48).

The old ways are out for Pier, but so are the new. When Pederson tries to persuade him to plow on the contour, he says, "Wal, I tell you, Pederson, I don't go much for them new fangled ideas." Another new-fangled idea he doesn't go for is reading; it is his refusal to learn to read that as much as anything else isolates him in the present.

Another man of the present, Blacktail, provides an interesting contrast to Pier. Their positions exactly reverse during the time of the action. In the opening scene, Pier, the young land owner off to get married, meets Blacktail, the down and out laborer who is drunk on the road after visiting the local whore. In the final scene, Blacktail, the wealthy land owner, is offering charity to Pier, the broken farmer who has lost both land and family. Perhaps the difference in their fortunes is in Blacktail's ability to read and to socialize.

Pier puts up an honest, respectable front, but his actions, Odysseuslike, hurt others; Blacktail puts up a bold, cynical front, but his actions often help others. Blacktail tells Pier when they meet on the road, "People are all crooks. . . . And my theory is to mink the other guy before he minks me" (16). Pier isn't prepared to differentiate between words and actions—to appreciate the ironical nature of Blacktail, who is a truthful rogue. Red Joe, Pier's good friend, does. He may not be able to farm as well as Pier, but he understands people better. He can tolerate Blacktail and even lets his son work for the man, much to Pier's chagrin.

Pier's feeling of suspicion and jealousy toward Blacktail is strangely parallel to Pier's feeling toward his son, Teo. Both represent a link to the future Pier has been denied. When Blacktail helps Teo with his interest in motors and machines, Pier is angry and jealous, even though he is proud of his son's ability for the advantage it gives him in farming. Pier's complex feelings toward both are revealed in the pig castrating episode. Uneasy about letting Teo and Red Joe's son watch the bloody process, Pier tries to keep them away. However, their natural curiosity is strong, and they persist, eventually causing Pier to cut his hand. In a playful gesture, Pier grabs Teo and throws him on his back in the operating trough, saying, "Get too close here and we're liable to grab you . . . an' take yers out by mistake instead" (197). But this by-play carries symbolic truth so powerful that even Pier senses it and feels especially guilty to have Blacktail appear just in time to witness the act. "It was like being caught at sacrificing a son, like an Abraham being caught with an Isaac on the altar" (198).

Nevertheless, Pier persists in what amounts to the castration of Teo by keeping him out of school, by making fun of his reading, and by trying to mold him into an image of himself. Teo's resentment builds up over the years until he sees himself a prisoner of farm work unable to escape. Finally, he gets up nerve to face Pier and tell him, "Dad, the trouble with you is, you keep picking things up by the heavy end. . . . You never stop to think things out. You rush into things too much. You figure everything's got to be done in a hurry. By bullin' it through. Maybe that was all right in old pioneer days. But not now." In the argument that follows, father and son almost come to blows, but Teo crashes his fist through the siding of the barn rather than hit Pier. "So I'm going. Going. And going for good. If you try to stop me, I'll just have to bust my way out," Teo shouts. Pier is finally ready to let him go and even to feel some envy (575).

Soon Pier, too, is on his own, free of farm and family. He has endured in spite of all, but he has not achieved the rewards of successful interaction with others. He is a flawed human being, and to that extent a tragic figure. Nertha says, "Sometimes I think I married a monster, a thing more beast, more bull, than man" (241). He may be bestial, but, like the Greek hero Odysseus, he chooses the hard way in spite of the pain he brings to himself and to others. To suffer and to cause suffering is the ultimate human quality, Homer leads us to believe. Pederson tells him, "It takes a hero to live out here and that's what you are" (604). At least he has a heroic ego, an individualism too strong to allow for social satisfaction. Manfred says, "An enlightened society is where strong individuals learn to tolerate each other as individuals. . . . I myself like to see a society of strong individualists who learn to get along" (C113 - 14).

C. *Social Criticism*

To learn to get along is what the people at that time needed, and Manfred is critical of two tendencies which held back social development. One was the tendency to "go it alone," as Pier tried to do and lost all; the other is to "go it together," but in tightly knit and isolated ethnic groups, as his parents tried to do and lost.

Much of the disrespectful anger Pier expressed toward his parents is generated out of his desire to break out of the ethnic bounds they prescribed. Nertha is only one-quarter Norwegian, but Pier's parents are shocked at the loss of the pure Frisian line. Manfred's skillful use of the Frisian language, and his insertion of the Frisian folklore, give authenticity to the emotional struggle Americanization can be. Part of Pier's tragedy is that he is caught between two societies—the Frisian, from which he wants to escape, and the fully Americanized, which he doesn't trust any more than he trusts Blacktail. This limbo is best symbolized in his inability to read—he won't talk Frisian and he won't learn to read English. He stands strong but alone.

This Is The Year received a balanced treatment from reviewers. While Walter Havinghurst in the *New York Herald Tribune Book Review* (3/23/47) was bored with endlessly detailed farm chores and rambling barnyard conversations, the *Time* (3/31/47) reviewer was pleased with the descriptions of farm chores such as plowing, cultivating, reaping, and threshing. However, he did feel that the conservation lesson was pushed too hard.

Nona Balakian in the *New York Times Book Review* (3/31/47) praised Manfred's word pictures, his accuracy of observation and intensity of sensation, but she felt that the characters lacked an "inner life to bring them close to us." Mark Schorer, in the *Kenyon Review* for Autumn 1947, felt the novel to be less art than an "unexplored

lump of experience," and the *New Yorker* (3/39/47) reviewer
thought Manfred gave altogether too much attention to the details
of farm life.

On the other hand, Roy Meyer, in his book *The Midwestern
Farm Novel*, sees Manfred's characterization of Pier as "convincing
and consistent." He writes: "The ignorant, stubborn, and yet
thoroughly human Pier Frixen. . . perhaps comes closer to the
stuff of real character portrayal than any other personality in recent
farm fiction." Meyer sees the book as a mixture of realism and
mysticism, coarseness and poetry, of bathos and beauty.[10]

III   The Chokecherry Tree *(1948)*

The intersection of U.S. Highways 75 and 18 in northwestern
Iowa is Perkins Corners, the setting for *The Chokecherry Tree*. It is
one of those major highway intersections which attracts gasoline
stations to its four corners. Two miles to the east is Hull, where
Manfred attended high school, and six miles to the northwest is
Doon, where he was born. The chokecherry tree of the title is gone
now, and the last of the thirteen mighty cottonwoods may soon go
because it is a traffic hazard. This is Manfred country, and *The
Chokecherry Tree* is a humorous book about home folks, good
times, and how Elof Lofblom got his "corner" on life.

In *The Chokecherry Tree* Frederick Manfred has given us an essentially comic figure in Elof Lofblom, a little man who escapes
tragedy through a noble acceptance of life. As we follow him
through his initiation trials, in a very different sequence of events
from those followed by Conquering Horse on this same prairie a
century earlier, we come to know Siouxland and its people—at least
those centered around Hello (Hull), Iowa, and nearby Chokecherry
Corner (Perkins Corners). There is, in fact, a documentary flavor to
the novel, supported to some extent by the choric chapter headings,
in which the author speaks for his protagonist, who is incapable of
revealing himself. As Manfred writes in the heading for Chapter
Eleven: "Elof, the only one capable of putting into writing the true
pit of your self is yourself. Yet, the moment you become capable of
doing so, you are no longer Elof[11]."

The "hope to live" is sometimes expressed by Manfred as the
"going on." In the headings for Chapters Eight and Nine (87, 98)
he equates "this momentum that drives us on" with a noncom-
bative voice of hope, a "voice as of a struggling God." In the follow-

ing chapter, Elof has not yet felt that hope and seems to be caught
in a circle of toil not unlike that imposed upon Sisyphus, who faced
an eternity of rolling a huge rock up a hill again and again.

He felt himself invaded by massive black-tipped waves of gray. Nothing
to look forward to but toil, toil, toil. Nothing on the horizon but a hateful
day weighted with hated slavery.
What a life.
He couldn't understand why he didn't rebel. Couldn't understand it. (99)

By the time Elof has passed through the several failures in love
and business that are his lot, he has come around to a happier frame
of mind. The toil, toil, toil is still ahead of him, but he has come to
accept himself for what he is. He still can't articulate it, but he
senses it. In the night after his fight with Gert and his reconciliation
with his father, he wakes and wonders at the meaning in the way his
arms and hands have fallen protectively at his crotch and breast.
"Blinking, he wondered what his Old Adam wanted from him this
night. . . . His feet tingled. They wanted to run, to jump. Or
something" (269).

We might wonder what he has to be happy about, just as we
might be in wonder at the interpretation Camus gives to Sisyphus in
his essay on the myth. Camus writes: "The struggle itself toward
the heights is enough to fill a man's heart. One must imagine
Sisyphus happy."[12]

Elof does not understand the mystery, the Old Adam in him, nor
does he need to. Such understanding is not of the intellect. Manfred
speaks for him in the heading to Chapter Nineteen:

One thing troubles us. To have survived the numbing discovery that you
were a simpleton and not a hero, to have discovered within yourself
courage enough to come home to certain abuse and ridicule—could it be
that a special quality resides in you after all? That we, pompous and lofty,
and warbling with a fancy tongue, are blind to it? That intellect, which we
worship just a little more than we fear, and consider our only hope, is as
heady a drink as religion? Is as much an opium? To have survived that double strain is perhaps the true hero's toil. . . . (246)

In placing this emphasis on the intuitive, as well as in his celebration of acceptance, Manfred sides with the existentialists and at the
same time with the primitivists. The existentialists would have us
consider the whole man: mind, body, and spirit. The primitivists

would have us consider man the whole, the participant in the
rhythm of the total universe. In this respect, Manfred may not only
be showing the influence of D. H. Lawrence and Walt Whitman,
but would appear to be anticipating such modern explorers of consciousness as Theodore Roszak, Marshall McLuhan, Rollo May,
Alan Watts, and Joyce Carol Oates.

Can a figure as inept as Elof, as pitiful, as unimaginative, as com-
ical, carry the universal overtones? Can he represent the human
condition? In a number of symbolic gestures, Manfred links Elof
with universal images of mediocrity—natural, physical, and literary.
The most significant nature image is the stunted chokecherry tree
with its bitter fruit, dominated by the large cottonwoods. Domina-
tion is reflected also in a pastoral scene where Elof sympathizes with
a young bull calf which is being knocked about by the old bull. Elof
is being "bullied" by his father, but the image is stretched further
so that the "killer bulls" come to be seen as world leaders who
destroy the Elofs as well as the Manfreds. In a strange and perhaps
inappropriate chapter, Manfred writes a letter for Elof protesting
war, with a salutation as follows: "Dear Mr. President (and all the
above mentioned Horned Bulls):" These were the other world
leaders.

Physical images of mediocrity are associated with Elof's body. He
is plagued with a large toe shorter than his second toe, said to be a
sign that he will never be dominant at home; and he is embarrassed
in the locker room by his small penis. His feet, shod in oversized
shoes, make a clown of him.

There are also literary images of mediocrity. Throughout the
book, Elof is trying to finish reading Smollett's *Peregrine Pickle*.
Both Peregrine and another Smollett hero, Roderick Random, are
Eloflike. In the preface to *Roderick Random*, Smollett writes that he
"attempted to represent modest merit struggling with every difficulty to which a friendless orphan is exposed."[13] Some significance
may be seen in the fact that unknown horses win in a carnival race
Elof attends in South Dakota. The winners are named Arabia Deser-
ta and Dawn in Britain, names of books by Charles Doughty, a little
read British writer who is a favorite with Manfred. The more
famous literary names are left behind.

In fact, the most serious criticism to be leveled at Elof is that he is
unworthy of our attention, that he is trivial or even subhuman. Yet
an Elof figure is not unique in literature. It is as modern as Arthur
Miller's Willie Loman in *Death of a Salesman* and as primitive as
Frank Waters' Martiniano in *The Man Who Killed the Deer*.

A comparison to the Waters novel about Pueblo Indian life might help to explain the role played by Elof's father. One reviewer complained that the father seemed "hazy," his bitterness as unaccounted for as his sudden capitulation to normal parental concerns. In the Waters novel, the Indian Martiniano, the man who killed the deer, is an Elof who has had a touch of education outside the Pueblo and thus, in returning home, is caught in a culture clash with the "fathers" of the tribe. He has learned new ways and feels drawn toward civilization, yet the tribal ceremonies also hold him in a mystical way he cannot understand. He finally becomes a "blanket Indian" and follows the traditional customs, just as Elof accepts the life lead by his father in settling in Chokecherry Corner. Martiniano reflects, "Life . . . is a simple thing when once accepted wholly," as he settles into the traditional Indian routine.[14] It is this feeling of simple content that causes Elof to want to get up in the night and walk under the cottonwood trees—a reconciliation with the fathers. Fathers can be cruel, but they are also healers, as when Pa healed Elof's poisoned foot with an old remedy. It is quite natural for Elof's father, then, to respond to his son's return as a man by offering gifts and friendship. Elof's father might wish to join the Pueblo fathers in their chant:

> Do not despise the breath of your fathers,
> But draw it into your body.
> That our roads may reach to where the life-giving road
>   of our sun father comes out,
> That, clasping one another tight,
> Holding one another fast,
> We may finish our roads together,
> That this may be, I add to your breath now.[15]

In seeing Elof as a transitional figure between the generation of his father and his own generation, one can tolerate certain inconsistencies in his character. De Boer sees Elof as sometimes too richly philosophical and then on the other hand sometimes too crude in his language and behavior.[16] Elof can outsmart the oil company representatives and reject his parents' religion, yet he holds on to a fear of hell and seems content with simple pleasures and crude humor. Nor can he finish reading *Peregrine Pickle* or complete his accounting course. These paradoxical qualities identify him as a linking figure, one who leaves the home environment, goes beyond it, yet returns to sustain it and appreciate it. In the last line of the book, Manfred writes: "Elof, the leaf; Lofblom, the flowered leaf . . ." (270). The true hero may be the one who relates easily, if not dramatically, to the past and to the future and thus, as a leaf which falls back to nourish the mother tree, fosters the "going on" Manfred cherishes.

While it is true that Elof is not able to comprehend what is happening to him, any more than the Indian Martiniano can, at least he does act to give his life meaning. He is not like Willie Loman in Miller's play, whose tragedy is that he went through life unwilling to accept the worth of his own best talents in carpentry and masonry. Instead he followed not his own but another person's view of the good life. At least Elof is able to reject both the "hand of God" decree that he was chosen for great things and the temptations of the salesman's life. He does learn, and thus he escapes Willie Loman's tragic situation. Perhaps Elof is even happy.

When *The Chokecherry Tree* came out, reviews were mixed. Nash Burger in *The New York Times* (4/8/48) saw Manfred writing "bluntly and unabashedly" but with "complete understanding of his material, with love for his places and his people." Yet he, as well as Robert Heilman, in *Sewanee Review* for Autumn 1958, finds Elof's "subhuman" and "unpoetic" level not quite appropriate for so much attention being paid to his inner consciousness. They would have liked more humorous external action, which they feel Manfred handles well. Heilman wants more discipline from the author and feels that "a preoccupation with little men . . . necessarily leads to triviality." On the other hand, Nolan Miller, writing in *The Antioch Review* (Summer 1948), feels that Elof "keeps his special dignity" and has a kind of Tom Sawyer flavor that is wholesome. Richard Sullivan, in *The New York Times Review of Books* (4/11/48), found Elof "merry, awkward, clownish, and above all—touching." Of the novel, he writes: "It appears to be that regrettably rare thing, a novel written without a trace of faking or dodging or sweetening. . . ."

IV   The Man Who Looked Like the Prince of Wales *(1965)*[17]

During the seventeen years between publication dates of *The Chokecherry Tree* and *The Man Who Looked Like the Prince of Wales,* Manfred was busy mainly with his successful Buckskin Man Tales. Then in the late sixties, he turned his attention again to portraiture of Siouxland farm folks. Garrett in *The Man Who Looked*

Like the Prince of Wales based on a hired hand Manfred once knew; he is a person just the reverse of Elof. That is, where Elof had trouble because he did not attract girls or friends, Garrett is the sort of person whose physical beauty and appetites are more than he can handle.

Manfred's novella appears to be a simple "story as story," and yet its very simplicity perplexes. Is it a Grant Wood painting, an Iowa characterization? Or has the reader been handed a huge practical joke, as Garrett hands Bill Tamming a plug of tobacco fouled with urine? Or does it invoke the tragic emotions of pity and fear? Is man the victim of his appetites? Is the individual a victim of society and tradition? Are there duplicates of each of us in the world?

Garrett Engelking and the Prince of Wales, Edward VIII or later Duke of Windsor, seem to be brothers in their blond good looks and their easygoing manner. The fact that the Englekings came from East Friesland makes the family think that these two might be related. But Ma doesn't see much point to the comparison: "Well, a lot a good it's done Garrett to look like him. It's got him into nothing but trouble, that's a fact."[18]

Whether prince or pauper, the "trouble" the man can get into through his good looks and his emotional drives is shattering. The prince gives up the crown of England, and the pauper is exiled from Siouxland to California to die away from home. But who is to blame? Free's father, Alf Alfredson, seems to find all the answer necessary in the often repeated, "The trouble with Garrett is, he can't leave it alone." His good looks alienate the men and attract the women, so that Garrett does not have to be an initiator. He merely has to say "no." But this is precisely what he cannot do, whether it be to women or to those who want credit or to liquor. He could have saved June, his first love, by saying "no" when she wanted to keep her pregnancy secret. And he could have said "no" to the church elders who insisted on humiliating him and then on denying him adopted children. Unlike Cain, of *Riders of Judgment*, Garrett isn't able to curb the animal within him, nor is he able to throw off the inhumane practices of the church and the community. He is thus victim both of his inheritance and of his environment, caught in a naturalistic trap. Even though Garrett may not be heroic enough to be a tragic figure, a certain amount of "pity" and "fear" can be generated over him. There but for the accident of birth go we, and our deaths could be as inappropriate, as accidental, as his. Furthermore, as with Garrett, our good qualities paradoxically turn

into weaknesses. Garrett would have been a great father, as the boy
Free knows, and he was kind, open, generous, unselfish, loving.
Why should he fail because of these good qualities? Do the good
guys always come in last? If so, there is reason to fear.

If all of the above seems too heavy for this little novella, it can be
taken as a realistic, even naturalistic, painting of small town Iowa
life in the early twentieth century. Reading through the short
chapters is not unlike watching home movies or colored slides of the
way it was: there are the baseball games, the buggy rides, the Saturday nights down town, the church gatherings, the farm work, and
the love making. However, the kind of realistic detail Manfred
provides for the love-making scenes would never be seen in home
movies.

A rustic humor and a joking tone permeate the novella even at its
most serious moments. During the cross-examination by the church
elders, the preacher takes time to tell a long story about a woman
who unraveled her husband's underwear during a service and
another of a boy who threw a paper wad into a snoring man's
mouth. A whole chapter is devoted to narrating a single practical
joke. These episodes may be seen as tragic relief, as playing to a pit
audience, or as part of a larger leg pull which some have seen the
novella to be. It certainly was no joking matter, though, to someone
in Manfred's home town of Doon, Iowa, where the story is set. After
the book's publication, someone there smeared creosote over the
sign proclaiming Doon as the birthplace of novelist Frederick Manfred.

The home town folks didn't appreciate Manfred's story any more
than the residents of Bonnie liked Garrett, but both found some
success in California. Helen V. Fowler of the *Los Angeles Times*
(1/23/66) was quite taken with the novella. It was she who saw it as
a Grant Wood portrait, but she also thought its characterizations
were as distorted as a Dali watch, in which the distortion is the real
image. "The beauty of the novel," she writes, "is in the frequently
occurring little gems of almost poetic writing."

While Helen V. Fowler was able to develop empathy for Garrett,
John K. Sherman in the *Minneapolis Tribune* (9/26/65) writes,
"There isn't enough substance in him to draw much sympathy or
concern from the reader." Sherman found that the explicit description of sex acts turned the reader into a Peeping Tom, but he praised Manfred's evocation of Siouxland people and his provocative imagery. John Milton, in the *Saturday Review* (11/6/65), praised

Manfred's sensitive touch with the land, but he felt the resemblance to the Prince of Wales was "neither pointed enough for a short story nor important enough for a novel." The hints of the tragic and poetic, he felt, were an attempt to do more than the novel could convey.

V   Eden Prairie (1968)

When Manfred wanted an image of pure innocence for a novel about the prairie as Garden of Eden, he turned to his Aunt Kathryn for a model. She was once his country school teacher and the first person to encourage him to be a writer. Manfred reports that when his Aunt Kathryn died in 1977, he found in her home a box containing all of his books in mint condition. They obviously hadn't been read. After becoming furious with the seduction scene in *The Golden Bowl*, she refused to read his books, thinking something was wrong with him. He was surprised, therefore, to find that she not only had bought the books but had kept a scrapbook about his career.[19] Thus, Kathryn as Karen in *Eden Prairie* provides a sharp contrast to Garrett in the previous novel, for innocence was not one of his virtues. The two novels point out dangers in both extremes of behavior.

In the poetic opening paragraph of *Eden Prairie*, Manfred describes the flight and death of two sulphur butterflies. As we meet Karen Alfredson and Konstant Harmer, we realize that they are human butterflies almost too delicate to mate and survive. They are innocents in a Siouxland eden in the early 1920s. Karen is raised by the Hamilton family in Bonnie when her family moves away. As she goes through high school, the intrusion of animal nature disturbs her innocence and health to the point that she falsely accuses a doctor of rape when he gives her a routine examination. When her menstrual period begins, her health returns and she takes a job as a country school teacher. She is shocked by the vulgarity of her students, but finds friendly help from a neighboring male teacher, Konstant Harmer, a match for her in delicacy.

Kon Harmer contrasts sharply with the masculine vulgarity of his brother, Charlie, the first born, but he shares a loving relationship with his brother Brant, the second born. When Kon and Karen decide to marry, Brant feels that Kon has let him down, even though his wife Mildred has given him a good home. Brant's mental condition degenerates; he fears witchcraft and takes his own life when he hears that Kon and Karen are expecting a baby. The baby is born dead, but Kon and Karen find the natural bond between them strengthened.

Eden Prairie illustrates the theme of the "fortunate fall" by showing pure innocence to be unnatural and destructive of human values. Kon and Karen are able to consummate their love for the first time only after watching and learning as their dog Wolf mates with a neighbor bitch. Their unnatural innocence is contrasted with Charlie's unnatural vulgarity, neither extreme being shown as desirable. Brant's wife, Mildred, represents the nearest approach to the fully normal balance favored by Manfred. She has an earthy attractiveness to the masculine, yet she is capable of loving and being faithful to Brant, who is flawed.

The contrast between innocence and vulgarity, between spirit and flesh, between the idyllic Iowa landscape and the sordid events that happen within it, sets up a tension which Manfred exploits for both comic and tragic effects. Karen in her absurd primness is more to be laughed at than pitied; whereas Brant, caught between the Adamic Kon and the devilish Charlie, resorts to suicide when he cannot find acceptance.

In being a second son, Brant feels rejected. His older brother Charlie takes after his father and is a successful farmer; his younger brother Kon is a favorite who is groomed for the "finer things," such as the ministry, teaching, music, or poetry. Manfred's early notes for the novel give the "second son" theme strong play as an exploration of what Manfred sees as a typical problem among farm families. The second son often simply waited in the wings for something to happen to his brothers. Brant, never happy, was most fulfilled through his friendship with Kon, a relationship threatened by the marriage of Kon and Karen.

Brant's love for his brother Kon is not ridiculed by Manfred. Rather, it is shown to be somehow natural and parallel to the male-female affair between Kon and Karen. In a flashback episode where Brant saves Kon from drowning while they are picking plums on an idyllic afternoon, Manfred has Brant say to Kon, both of whom are naked while their clothes are drying, "I wish we could try standing back to back close together once and at the same time I could throw my arms around you"[20]. The image here recalls the passage from Plato's *Symposium* in which Aristophanes explains the history and nature of man:

For at first there were three sexes, not two as at present, male and female, but also a third having both together; the name remains with us, but the thing is gone. . . . Next the shape of man was quite round, back and ribs passing about it in a circle; and he had four arms and an equal number of legs, and two faces on a round neck, exactly alike; there was one head with these two opposite faces, and four ears, and two privy members, and the rest you might imagine from this.[21]

As Aristophanes explains it, the androgynous humans were powerful and ambitious to the point of attacking the gods themselves. So Zeus and the other gods decided that, rather than kill the tribe of man, they would slice each human down through the middle—thus making men weaker and at the same time more useful because there would be more of them.

Through this splitting of each of the three sexes, mutual love was implanted in mankind, since each half tends to seek its other self. Aristophanes says that all men who are a cutting of the manwoman sex are fond of women, and all women cut from that sex are mad for men. The women who are a cutting of the ancient women do not care much about men, but are more attracted to women. Those males who are a cutting of the male pursue the male.

If on the one hand Manfred speaks for manly men and womanly women, at the same time he stresses acceptance and toleration of deviations, as Mildred accepts and loves Brant. Karen frequently defends her unique personality with such expressions as, "Well, I don't care. I have a right to be left alone." With these words she might well be speaking for the beautiful butterflies of the opening passage. They are destroyed, just as the innocence of Karen and Kon is destroyed—raped—by a world that seems to have no place for them.

In his review for *Western American Literature* (Winter 1969), Max Westbrook praises the novel for the power it gives to both viewpoints—to the factual world of the doctor and to the unreal world of the innocent. However, some reviewers of *Eden Prairie* have been critical of the crudities Manfred sets in opposition to the innocence of the Garden, one accusing him of being an Erskine Caldwell in the wheatfields because of the "privy" humor. The reviewer in *Publisher's Weekly* commented on Manfred's "original and often startling way of dropping a blunt crudity, like a grub, into a passage of creamy and fairly bland prose;" and on his ability to shift from lovely nature scenes into the worst corner of the barnyard without blurring the focus (7/15/68). The tension between these opposites gives a certain power to the novel, making it both grim and beautiful. Manfred says it is a favorite of his.

CHAPTER 3

Searching for an American Self: Tales

THE first five books discussed in this section make up the Buckskin Man Tales, arranged in the order they were written. However, according to Manfred's program for presenting slices of life in Middle America during the nineteenth century, they would have the following chronological order: (1) *Conquering Horse*—Indian prewhite times in 1800; (2) *Lord Grizzly*—mountain man times in 1823 - 1824; (3) *Scarlet Plume*—Sioux uprising in 1862; (4) *King of Spades*—Black Hills justice in 1876; (5) *Riders of Judgment*—cattlemen times in 1892. The sixth tale, *The Manly-Hearted Woman*, was not a part of the original design but is characteristic of the "tale." It would fit into the time period of *Conquering Horse*.

Russell Roth sees the unifying theme of the Buckskin Man Tales as "the search for the true self in a context of an evolving and generic *American* self."[1] He points out that there is a natural progression from the last of James Fenimore Cooper's Leatherstocking Tales, *The Prairie*, to *Conquering Horse*, first of the Buckskin Man Tales. Both books deal with the same time period and have the Pawnees in their plots. At the other end of the century, as Roth points out, the Buckskin Man Tales, ending as they do with *Riders of Judgment* and the move from cattle to crops, lead naturally to Manfred's "farm" novels, particularly *The Golden Bowl* and *This is the Year*. The "search for the true self" that Roth writes of requires a character to reject his old European consciousness in favor of a new "American" personality.[2]

Jacque Pruett agrees with Roth in seeing the theme of the tales as the search for identity, but she also believes each tale suggests that "Western man can save himself by combining with the Indians' harmonious relationship with the land his own inherent resourcefulness and drive."[3] She suggests that the "white girl Indian-raised" or the offspring of Bending Reed and Hugh Glass might represent the ideal combination. She writes:

Manfred implies through the thematic inter-relationship of the Buckskin
Man Tales that the stability and inherent beauty of No Name's world is
available also to the white man, but there remains the inability of the man
in the West to see his rightful place with respect to the earth and other
men. Of the white men in these stories, only Hugh Glass manages to get
completely in phase with the universe and thus he is saved.[4]

Hugh Glass is saved almost in spite of himself through a mystical
experience. Manfred may well be suggesting in these tales that
Western man's almost total emphasis on reason, while it has enabled him to conquer nature in many ways, has also denied him a
sacred harmony with that nature.

The symbol for this white man obsessed with reason, according to
Mick McAllister, may be seen in the Protestant concept of Jehovah,
a figure lonely, solitary, childless, unwedded, and unloved. In a
paper presented before the Western Literature Association in October 1977, McAllister writes:

This god stalks through the Buckskin Man Tales, gradually supplanting
the indigenous spirits of the land. The Buckskin Man Tales are about the
warring of gods and religions, the supplanting of the true hunter and
wearer of skins with the false Esau. The final result of the cosmic combat
established in *Conquering Horse* and played out in the trivial human lives
of the following novels is the tragic, apocalyptic victory of that Protestant
Jehovah, God of Abraham and Isaac.

He goes on to show how the story of Abraham and Isaac, including
Jacob and Esau, has a bearing on each of the Buckskin Man Tales.
The Bible, he says, has provided since our national beginnings the
justification we needed for raping the land and slaughtering her
people: "That god of Abraham and Isaac, of Jacob and Job, moves
like a mad father through the Buckskin Man Tales, slaying his sons
and imposing his death-directed will upon the living land."

Thus, McAllister sees Manfred as writing in the Buckskin Man
Tales a deeply moral but pessimistic statement about the westering
movement.[5]

I   Lord Grizzly *(1954)*

By every measurement, *Lord Grizzly* stands as Manfred's most
successful novel thus far. It has brought to him both monetary
reward and critical acclaim. It is what he wanted it to be: his own

Odyssey, an original which "would not strictly follow any allegory or plot already recorded, but would follow what Glass and America would demand as prototypes in their own right."[6]

Manfred may have been inspired by the Hugh Glass story to strike out himself in a new direction at a time when his fortunes were down. He took the radical step of changing his name from Feike Feikema, and he launched an ambitious series of tales much more historical than anything he had written previously. Thus, the "Frederick Manfred" identity begins with *Lord Grizzly;* it is an American name pointing back to father Hugh.

Hugh Glass, a fifty year old mountain man serving under General Ashley on the Missouri River, escapes with his life in an Indian raid and recuperates in nearby Ft. Kiowa in South Dakota, where he is reunited with his Indian wife, Bending Reed. He leaves again soon with a party of thirteen, under the command of Major Henry, to get fur in the Rocky Mountains. Young Jim Bridger and book-read "Fitz" Fitzgerald make up the advance hunting party. When Jim and Fitz sleep while on guard, Hugh lies for them. Major Henry orders Hugh to shave his beard, but Hugh refuses and goes off to hunt alone. He is attacked by a mother grizzly bear with cub and is badly mauled, but the bear is killed.

When he awakes, he finds his wounds stitched, but Fitz and Jim are gone. He sets his broken leg and crawls, dragging one leg on a travois, toward Ft. Kiowa. He helps an old squaw and has narrow escapes from Indians, buffalo, and a bear, but his hatred for Fitz and Jim keep him going until he reaches the Cheyenne River. He builds a dugout canoe and floats back to Ft. Kiowa.

Again Bending Reed nurses him to health, and again he heads out—this time as part of a keel boat crew headed up river to Ft. Tipton. He wants to find and kill Jim and Fitz for leaving him alone to die. When only he escapes alive in an attack on the keel boat, Hugh believes that the Lord has chosen him to seek revenge. He sets out alone for Henry's new post, where he finds Jim. They fight to a draw. When Jim explains that he and Fitz had to run when attacked by Indians, Hugh reprieves him but goes on in search of Fitz. He leads a group of four men with a message for Ft. Atkinson. All but Hugh, who hides in a snake pit, are killed by Ree Indians. Hugh goes on alone and sees a "ghost" bear following him, but he makes it safely to Atkinson and signs on there as hunter. Fitz eventually arrives, and Hugh, after counting his own faults, forgives both Fitz and Jim.

Only a consummate artist could give us a work so original, which, nevertheless, is about a historical figure and which carries about it the aura of man's heritage in the Greek, biblical, European, Indian, and Western American cultures and gives the sense of man's psychological underpinning in his animal nature.

A. *History*

Lord Grizzly packs a strong literary wallop because it is built on a foundation of solid historical fact and personal experience, while at the same time it transcends these in its allusions and in its mystical and mythic overtones.

Hugh Glass was a man, an American, our ancestor. As such he was just the figure Manfred needed to add another kind of dimension to his writing, to represent a "usable past" in primitive origins. In *Conversations*, Manfred says, "I thought the characters in my books up to that point were two-dimensional. . . . There was a background missing in all of them. So I became interested in the *Lord Grizzly* idea . . . because I wanted to dig into our past history out there"(68).

And dig he did, reading over two hundred pieces relating to the Glass legend, research documented in the University of Minnesota Archives, where his working notebook for *Lord Grizzly* is preserved. Starting with the story as found in a *South Dakota Guide* (Pierre, 1938), he read such books as Hiram M. Chittenden's *The American Fur Trade of the Far West*, George F. Ruxton's *Life in the Far West*, George Catlin's *North American Indians*, and Sir James Frazer's *The Golden Bough*.

From early newspaper accounts and from the chronicles of George C. Yount, Manfred pieced together the basic history of Hugh Glass, which is retold and expanded upon in *Lord Grizzly*. An important reference was an unsigned sketch, probably by James Hall, in the Philadelphia *Port Folio*, entitled "The Missouri Trapper." These sources provided a rather consistent outline of the Glass history: his early years in Pennsylvania, his days as a sailor, his capture by pirates, his escape and capture by the Pawnees, his life with them, his escape and work for Ashley as a trapper, his fight with the bear, and his death in battle with Indians.

Manfred says he thought of using the story of John Colter or Jim Bridger but chose Hugh Glass because Glass had no ulterior motives. He did not go in for money, family, the military, or religion but simply acted because Major Henry told him not to. He saw Glass as one who lived for an idea or an ideal—at first maybe it was revenge, but then compassion—and this purpose represented for Manfred the ultimate human goal (C106 - 107).

But Glass the man could not have articulated such purposes, and Manfred needed to know more than what the books and articles could tell him. He had to feel the territory himself and know the truth about the inner experience. Before he started writing, he had read and collected data for ten years. In *Conversations*, he tells about his walking over Hugh's crawl route in central South Dakota, collecting specimens of plants and bugs and getting a feel for the country as Hugh might have experienced it. On this trip, he talked to storekeeper Arthur Svenby in Lemmon about local history and visited with Albert Simpson, a seventy-three-year old Ree medicine man.[7] After he got home, he built a travois for himself like the one Hugh made for his broken leg and then crawled over his acreage to see how it would feel. "In filling it all out you might as well have it true rather than false," he explains (C71).

In getting at this truth, Manfred tried to identify himself physically with Hugh. In the *Lord Grizzly* notebook he writes: "He [Hugh] is 55, with such aches and pains as I have come up with so far—still great power, quickness but wary, with short-windedness in running distances . . . aches in foot, shoulders, in his elbow and wrist, his gnarled hands. . . . He himself is a grizzly bear—gray, burly. . . ."[8]

Manfred, however, was not content to have only the physical truth, but wanted as well to sense the emotional truth of Hugh's forgiveness. In the flyleaf to the first edition, now in the University of Minnesota Archives, he explains that he couldn't figure out how to end the story until he himself had a forgiving experience: "I had to learn all three: to love, to hate, and to forgive." In *Conversations* he explains that the experience involved a brother who was falsely accused by the state. The state had to apologize, and the brother could have sued, but he did not. He forgave the state. "When I saw this in front of me, I then knew how to end it. Emotionally. Truly" (C110).

B.   *Form and Rhythm*

Once Manfred had read his fill of Western lore, had exposed himself to the South Dakota environment, and had imaginatively gotten down to the "bare essentials," he was ready to write. "I want to know as much as I possibly can, consciously and intellectually about a subject. But when it comes time to write, then I turn my back on my more obvious knowledges. I turn my back on all previous theories on plot and previous theories on style, and I try to find the inner truth of what I am getting at" (C109). As he began to write, the forms and rhythms and symbols began to emerge, somehow, out of the process of writing.

One of the rhythmic patterns that emerged was the Old Testament configuration of threes, most obvious in the three parts of the book, titled "The Wrestle," "The Crawl," and "The Showdown." The number three, according to J. E. Cirlot, symbolizes spiritual synthesis and forms a half circle comprising birth, zenith, and descent.[9] From a psychologist's point of view, as explained by Ludwig Paneth, three also stands for biological synthesis and for the solution of a conflict.[10] These meanings of three are appropriate for the spiritual and biological synthesis that may be seen in *Lord Grizzly*. John R. Milton has identified the several levels on which the pattern of threes operates. The three parts of the book show Hugh Glass in a movement from membership in a group to an individual effort to survive, then back to group membership. Milton suggests, too, that in "The Crawl" there is a three step progression in Hugh, as in man, from animal level to human level to some kind of spiritual recognition. Physically, this would show Hugh and man developing in three stages—on the belly, on all fours, and upright. On the natural level, the lunar rhythm is quietly evident in the use of Indian names for months and in the three month length of important episodes. On a psychological level, Hugh is led toward compassion by watching as three mountain men, including Fitz, stagger into the fort from wilderness adventures. On the symbolic level, there are three bears—Hugh, the "White Grizzly"; the bear Hugh wrestles; and the phantom bear. As for style, Manfred often repeats phrases in units of threes, and in establishing point of view, he varies our point of observation from Hugh's mind (modified stream of consciousness), from Hugh's eyes (reader and Hugh perceive together), and from a third position just outside Hugh (limited omniscience).

Milton sees the psychical distance thus established as an important distinction of major Western novels, as opposed to the autobiographical novels which depend on emotional impact and vision. In novels like *Lord Grizzly*, the distance, the rhythm, and the form bear the meaning, Milton points out.[11]

One way in which meaning comes through form is in the repetition of patterns associated with other cultures and traditions. In *Lord Grizzly*, for instance, several layers of meaning are suggested in allusions to archetypal patterns in other literary works and to ceremonial motifs. Jacque Pruett has pointed out three patterns which work simultaneously in the novel: (1) the classic literary myth-quest adventure; (2) the Indian puberty rite, the ritual for achieving manhood; and (3) the death-rebirth cycle, as in the biblical crucifixion story.[12]

The flavor of knight errantry and the journey-quest motif is supplied through subtle references to Hugh as a "knight" in buckskin or as "Child Hugh," suggesting Byron's Childe Harold and Browning's Childe Roland. One can even see something of a Don Quixote in the final episode when Hugh rides the mule named Heyoka. Jacque Pruett shows that there is a close parallel between *Lord Grizzly* and *Sir Gawain and the Green Knight*. The journey, or "rite de passage," is one of suffering and testing in the wilderness to ascertain the hero's worthiness. Both the Green Knight and Hugh are brought to painful awareness of their human failings, including pride and cowardice, and achieve humility.[13]

More ancient journey patterns are suggested in references to the wanderings of Moses [14] and to Homer's *Odyssey* (118). The process by which the mountain man folklore is assimilated into poems, stories, and novels is similar to the process by which Homeric poems and Norse sagas were formed.[15] By using a traditional journey motif, Manfred builds meaning into the structure of the novel, for he suggests that each man's life is a process, a movement, perhaps a crawling movement, toward spiritual development. Manfred seems to be suggesting, too, that as each man's life follows this pattern, so the human animal as a species has followed a natural progression upward. Hugh lives like an animal during the crawl but evolves from a "crawling whangdoodle" to a walking man.[16]

In addition to the journey motif, Indian and Christian religious rites provide a structural base for the novel. The pattern of *Lord Grizzly* can be compared to the pattern of *Conquering Horse*, which is a book closely following the Indian ritual for achieving manhood. The hero is cleansed by fasting in order to receive a vision which reveals his guardian, the spirit of an animal. The hero then withdraws from the tribe for a time in order to undertake the deeds prescribed in the vision, which may include killing the sacred animal from which his "medicine" is prepared. The warrior then returns to the tribe, receives his new name, and is welcomed as a true brave. Hugh follows very nearly this same three step pattern. His vision comes only after he has proven himself worthy by his bravery and by overcoming his stubborn pride; he goes through a trial in isolation, and he is reborn both physically and spiritually. [17]

There is a strong parallel also to the death and rebirth cycle in the crucifixion story. Hugh starts out with twelve companions, two of whom betray him. When Hugh sets his leg, he must bear "inhuman pain," as does Christ on the cross. He is in the wilderness for three months, a month for each day between crucifixion and resurrection. He is tempted as was Christ to despair. In Part III he must stay in a snake pit for three days with a stone over the opening. He feels betrayed and sees the reward as Judas money (276). He weeps over Old Mother and his dead boys as Christ over Lazarus. Hugh refers to another ascension three times during the story (11, 200, 253).

C. Style

In addition to providing meaning through structure, Manfred uses stylistic devices to support the lines of meaning. Indian, mountain man, and Old Testament phrases and usages come together unobtrusively to support the universality of the themes. An examination of Manfred's Lord Grizzly notebook shows how carefully the mountain man language was authenticated from such sources as Ruxton's Life in the Far West and Garrard's Wah-to-yah and the Taos Trail.

Repetition is used in a number of ways to support themes and to unify the story. Milton sees the repetition in opening lines to the eight sections of "The Crawl" as paralleling a progression in the plot. "A cold nose woke him" is repeated in the early stages of the crawl, but the line changes toward the end to "Hugh climbed steadily" and finally to "Wild geese were flying south." Milton suggests that the lines show progression from the animal instinct to survive to human feelings of revenge, which are supplanted by a spiritual victory in forgiveness. [18]

Pruett has pointed out Manfred's repeated use of "gray" in Chapter I as a means of linking Hugh and the grizzly together. Although repetition sometimes gets out of hand, as in too many repetitions of similar subject-verb combinations, the repetition of "forgot," as Pruett points out, is effective in showing the kind of intoxication induced by a buffalo hunt:

Hugh forgot himself, forgot he had a game leg, forgot he'd ever loved, forgot he'd ever killed Rees or any other kind of red devil, forgot he'd ever been a buccaneer killing Spanish merchantmen, forgot he was the papa of two boys back in Lancaster, forgot he'd ever deserted the boys because of their rip of a mother, forgot all, forgot he was Hugh even, forgot both Old Hugh and Young Hugh, was lost in the glorious roaring chase, killing killing killing—all of it a glorious bloodletting and complete forgetting. (60)

Not only does this paragraph capture some feel for the hunt, but it very concisely summarizes Hugh's life and, in a "bloodletting" ceremony, explains both the attractions and the vulgarities inherent in his chosen way. After the hunt Hugh will remember, and in remembering the incidents listed in the paragraph, he will find self-knowledge and humility which will lead him toward compassion.

Repetition is a biblical device, especially the pattern of threes, and in *Lord Grizzly* there are echoes of the Old Testament style, particularly that of the "Song of Solomon." Even such a short line as "he wept" has an important allusion to John 11:35 in view of the symbolism Manfred has established. In a letter to James Austin, Manfred explains how he wrote *Lord Grizzly:*

I can say, however, that to help myself write it, to get the feel of an olden time, my thoughts quite naturally went back to the Old Testament, which I heard read, and which I read myself, every day three times a day for some 17 years before I left for college. It also seemed to me that Indian life and mountain man life was in many ways very much like the tribulations of the heroes of the Old Testament. I also thought of the Old Greeks, the Old Romans, and of course I did enormous amounts of reading in *The Golden Bough* and other like studies of our mystery-shrouded ancestry. And then, reading, brooding, I sat back and listened for what I might hear from far inside myself. After exhausting all reasonable approaches to the problem, I then listened for "instinct" or the "inner voice" or the "Old Leviathan" or the "Old Lizard" to speak. It or he knows. [19]

In rhythm, form, and style, then, *Lord Grizzly* reflects Greek, biblical, European, and Indian cultures. Similarly, these influences overlay the thematic and symbolical aspects of the novel.

D. *Symbol and Theme*

When Manfred speaks of the "Old Lizard" in the quotation above, he might have used the term "Old Eph" as well, for the bear

in alchemy corresponds to the "nigredo" of prime matter and hence
is related to all initial stages and to the instincts. According to J. E.
Cirlot, it has been considered a symbol of the perilous aspect of the
unconscious and an attribute of the man who is cruel and crude.
The bear is regarded as a lunar animal since it is found in the company of Diana.[20] Hugh, as we first know him, is cruel and crude,
and he is associated throughout the book with moonlight and silver,
especially on the crawl and later when he sees the "haunt" grizzly.

Manfred's use of "old Eph" as a symbol of the animal may be
compared to Faulkner's use of the bear "old Ben" in his story "The
Bear." Both Manfred and Faulkner show how man as animal shares
possession of the land with the bear, identifies with him, and yet
reaches beyond. From the opening pages of *Lord Grizzly*, we are
led to think of Hugh in "grizzly" terms. "There was about him too
the lonesome aggrieved mien of the touchy old grizzly bear. . ."
(7). He has a "grizzly leathery face" (34), and his hair, sometimes
called fur, is gray and thick as that of an animal. He won't shave.
He humps his neck and growls his replies to Major Henry (83).
Even his voice is gruff, the result of a throat wound, so he is able to
imitate a bear roar and scare off wolves and buzzards (101).

While Hugh's Indian name is "White Grizzly," Manfred's title is
"Lord Grizzly," so there is from the start an implication that the
bear has "lordly" qualities and, by symbolic association, that Hugh
as a bear of a man has these qualities also. According to bear lore as
reported in *The Golden Bough*, in the North the bear is seen either
as a god or as messenger of the gods.[21] Major Henry takes Hugh's
part in defending the grizzly by telling how a tribe he knows, before
they kill the bear, bring him their best food, bow to him, and ask
forgiveness "for what they are about to do," saying they know he
wants to die for them. "It almost reminds me, it does, of the way
the white man, the civilized man, has treated his Lord and Master,
Jesus Christ. Civilized man had to kill him too, crucify him even,
before he could become their giver of life" (73).

Hugh begins to carry a heavy symbolic load. He has the strength
and bearing of an animal, the intelligence and pride of a superior
human being—Indian, knight errant, chief, or Old Testament
prophet, or King of the Jews. Bending Reed's treatment of Hugh as
"lord and master" is both in the Indian tradition, as she rubs him
with bear grease, and in the Old Testament tradition of anointing
the body with oil. James Austin has written about the many
allusions to the King James Bible in which Manfred compared

Hugh to two biblical heroes: Samson in the forward and Samson's killing of the lion, from the body of which came forth honey (Judges 14:5 - 14); to Samson's hair, as well as Esau's, and the selling of a birthright (I Samuel 10:1, 16:13); to Jacob, who fought with the angel and was injured in the leg and who bequeaths his right to the promised land. Furthermore, Hugh has an Old Testament sense of justice. He often misquotes "an eye for a tooth and a tooth for an eye," (Leviticus 24:20 - 21), and he is obsessed with the idea that he is "chosen" to bring God's vengeance on the men who deserted him. He likes the idea that "the red devil has a code," strict as the old religion (154). It is old religion guilt that leads him, in remembering his own desertion of family and of Bending Reed, to the new religion of Christian charity.[22]

Pruett reports that in an interview with Manfred, he said that he sees the Indians as America's first people and the period of their civilization as America's Old Testament; he sees the white man and his civilization as America's New Testament. In his notebook on *Lord Grizzly*, he wrote "Vengeance is mine is old talk by old people."[23]

The regeneration of Hugh from "eye for tooth" to Christlike forgiveness is subtly encouraged through his relationship with the bear, which is representative of both Christ and nature. Both Old Elph and Hugh achieve dignity through their relationship to the land. Hugh suffers in the wilderness and achieves his vision there. Hugh and the bear are one, as they appear to be during the wrestle. Hugh, in what amounts to communion or cannibalism, eats the bear to live, and thus he shares the bear's qualities. During the crawl, he is protected by using the bear's skin as his skin and, as the Indians believed, he thus can take over the bear's spirit. A bear shows him how to forgive when it licks the maggots from his wound. Pruett sees this act as a tacit message, as from Luke 11:37: "Go, and do thou likewise." By licking up the maggots, the bear purifies Hugh in body and spirit, for the maggots would turn into flies and serve as pests, outward symbols of Hugh's sins—akin to the pesting furies of Greek mythology. Thus cleansed, Hugh is ready to reach a Garden of Eden at the Cheyenne River, where he "restores his soul" as in the Twenty-Third Psalm.

As the spirit of the Lord, the bear teaches brotherhood and dies to save Hugh's soul. It arises again in the form of another grizzly which haunts Hugh on the White River. In *Conversations*, Manfred says:

I still don't know myself whether that was a real grizzly or a spiritual grizzly that was following Hugh down the White River. I don't know myself. There were days when I thought that I was really describing a real one. And there were days when I thought I was describing a haunt-like grizzly. And since it happened that way, it's precisely a good thing, because it sets up a wondering in the reader's mind. (C112)

Whichever it was, Hugh feels queer and senses that he is in a natural holy place. He sees his past life in four scenes and sees that pride, wealth, ambition, and theological systems all end in the grave. He does not understand the vision at the time, but it haunts him and prepares him for his reconciliation with Fitz.

However, as Austin points out, this reconciliation is symbolic of a greater reconciliation that Manfred feels should be the destiny of America. In Hugh three strains meet—the European, the primitive, and the animal. Austin writes:

It is thus that he can be both Jacob, the smooth one, and Esau, the hunter—both White Grizzly, the child of nature, and man, the killer of the grizzly and conqueror of nature. His character is formed as much by his attunement with nature as by his respect for the ways of the Indian or his civilized love of his comrades. [24]

In this respect, Hugh provides the third dimension Manfred was looking for in his characters—a usable past, a father figure that is peculiarly American, a new Adam, a new Odysseus. Hugh, of course, isn't aware of his role, nor does he understand that he has achieved freedom, but Manfred is aware and sees Hugh as D. H. Lawrence's "true American." Austin writes that Hugh thought that he came West for freedom, but in the end he found that true freedom came, as Lawrence says, from within: "Men are free when they are obeying some deep inward voice of religious belief. Obeying from within. . . . Not when they are escaping to some wild west." [25]

It may well be that Hugh is the "new American," the father of us all, but he is taught through echoes of his many pasts—Indian to Greek. The echoes of the past are especially important as the theme of vengeance is sublimated into the theme of tolerance and forgiveness. For example, there is a blending of "snake" and "Eden" imagery, with the Indian idea of justice through revenge. Pruett points out that the Indians' prayer "aid me in revenge," is similar to King David's song of praise, Psalm 18, "Thou hast also given me the necks of mine enemies; that I might destroy them that hate me." [26]

The revenge and treachery themes are established early in the novel, because the reason for the Indian attack is revenge for deaths in an earlier fight with white traders. Revenge is passed along, then, in the manner of a family curse in Greek tragedy. Stabbed, an Arikara brave, seeks revenge for Hugh's killing of his brother, Bear Mouth. It is Stabbed who scares Jim and Fitz away from Hugh, and it is Stabbed's vengeance again which causes the deaths of three of Hugh's men. At the very moments when Hugh is the victim of revenge, he himself has revenge in his heart. He sees the Indians as "onhuman varmits and need to be taught a lesson. Red Devils" (75). Later, during the showdown, Hugh says, "So this is how I'm practiced on, is it? Treachery and snakes all around" (222).

It is true that he is confronted with snakes all around—one sleeps by him, and he has to hide in a snake pit for three days. But, along with the snake is the Garden of Eden image of renewal and joy. When Hugh reaches the Cheyenne River, he has finally left behind the worrisome Thunder Butte, a reminder of his sins, and is able to shed his bear skin, as a snake sheds its skin. He has a new body, but not yet a new spirit. The new spirit comes following another experience in the "Garden" near Ft. Atkinson.

The paradox of the snake as both symbol of treachery and of self-knowledge is repeated in Manfred's use of the Indian god Heyoka, who possesses Bending Reed and causes her to be contrary. In Neihardt's *Black Elk Speaks,* the Heyoka ceremony is explained:

But in the heyoka ceremony, everything is backwards, and it is planned that the people shall be made to feel jolly and happy first, so that it may be easier for the power to come to them. You have noticed that the truth comes into this world with two faces. One is sad with suffering, and the other laughs; but it is the same face, laughing or weeping. When people are already in despair, maybe the laughing is better for them; and when they feel too good and are too sure of being safe, maybe the weeping is better for them to see. And so I think that is what the heyoka ceremony is for.[27]

Bending Reed, through Heyoka, is able to turn hatred to love and vengeance to compassion. She is Hugh's better self, and while under her influence he cannot kill his "boys." Her very name suggests tolerance and echoes Haemon's advice to his father in Sophocles' *Antigone:* "Seest thou, beside the wintry torrent's course, how the trees that yield to it save every twig, while the stiff-necked perish root and branch."[28]

General Ashley tries to remind Hugh of the same need to "bend" and asks, "Don't you have any feelings of kindness to go along with those feelings of hate? You have no forgiveness in you at all? You've never made a mistake you couldn't help?" (259) During his conversation with Hugh, a stubborn mule brays on the parade ground. The contrary animal is appropriately named Heyoka and thus continues to carry to Hugh the influence of Bending Reed. He is reminded of her also in the clothes he wears, sewn with her backward stitch. Thus Hugh is led, almost against his reason, to forgive Fitz and Jim, to bend from his individual stubbornness and to rejoin the group. "We boys" he can say at last (281).

In this way the themes of vengeance and forgiveness come together in the end, along with the theme of pride, the Greek hubris, the Indian fear of losing face. Hugh loses some pride when he sees three other mountain men come in from the West after a suffering equal to his own. And it is pride that keeps Fitz from telling the truth about the desertion. "Well, Hugh," Fitz says, "I must admit that there I made a mistake. I should have told that straight" (280). There is an interesting parallel situation in Hawthorne's short story, "Roger Malvin's Burial." Here, too, a man has been left alive to die, and the deserter refuses to admit his mistake. Hawthorne explains: "He regretted, deeply and bitterly, the moral cowardice that had restrained his words when he was about to disclose the truth to Dorcas; but pride, the fear of losing her affection, the dread of universal scorn, forbade him to rectify this falsehood."[29] Hawthorne suggests that the sin is not in leaving the person, but in refusing to admit it. This refusal is the sin of pride.

In Hugh Glass, Manfred has found a usable past to show us how to face the future, even though we may feel as confused as Hugh does when at the end he says, "Turned tame, this child has. Passed through such a passel of things he don't rightly recollect wrong from right no more" (281). His reason does not understand, but his "Old Lizard" knows how he should act. By following his inner voice, he has achieved freedom.

The overwhelmingly favorable reviews of *Lord Grizzly* reestablished Manfred's career under his new name, and with the novel's entry onto the best seller lists, his financial burdens were relieved. There were three printings in hard cover, leading to large paperback sales. In general, reviewers praised the novel's tight construction, its authentic language and history, and its allusions to our literary and mythological heritage.

William Carlos Williams wrote, "I have never in a lifetime of reading about our west met with anything like it. . . . It was a thrill. It held me spellbound from beginning to end as much by the skill of the writing as the intrinsic fascination of the story itself, which is phenomenal."[30]

A favorite word with the reviewers was "most":

"The most memorable of all frontier novels I have ever read," Roger Becket wrote in the *Long Island Sunday Press* (10/10/54).

"The most authentic account of frontier life ever written," according to R. Pearson in the *Minneapolis Star* (11/8/55).

"The most physiological novel ever written," Walter Havinghurst wrote in the *New York Herald Tribune Book Review* (11/28/54).

II   Riders of Judgment *(1957)*

In the historical sequence of the Buckskin Man Tales, *Riders of Judgment* comes last. Where *Conquering Horse* shows us what life was like at the beginning of the nineteenth century before the white man came to Siouxland, *Riders of Judgment* shows us the end of the century, when no Indians are evident. In between, the tales show us the ruthless elimination of the "wild" people and land. About all that is left of wildness in *Riders of Judgment* is the "animal" in Cain Hammett; and Hunt is bound to destroy even that. Mick McAllister sees Hunt as the personification of the white American spirit, called "The Puritan" by Frank Waters, which destroys the vitality of the Indian vision of openness to the land and to physical life, especially as encountered in sensual love.[31]

The loner, Cain Hammett, dominates *Riders of Judgment*. He throws in with the "little" cattlemen against the "big spread" boys and makes enemies of Jesse and Mitch, who work a big spread for Lord Peter Caudle. Cain and his wild brother, Harry, share the affection of Rory, wife of their easygoing brother, Dale. Rory fights with Dale because he will not kill outright an old enemy, Link Keeler (alias Hunt Lawton), who has killed both her father and Dale's. Mitch and Jesse heat up the cattle conflict by trying unsuccessfully to hang Harry and by actually hanging Avery and Queeny, a couple who had run a bar and had built up a small herd through Queeny's prostitution. When Dale is shot from ambush, probably by Hunt, Rory goads Cain to seek revenge; but he can't get Hunt to draw, and he rides Lonesome so hard that the horse dies. At spring roundup time, the small outfits organize, and the big operators plan a range war against them, claiming that they are rustlers. Cain, the target of their first attack, is ambushed at breakfast in his cabin. He holds them off for a day, but is finally burnéd out and shot. Harry escapes and sounds an alarm, so that the invaders are captured and jailed.

In talking about *Riders of Judgment* with John Milton in *Conversations*, Manfred said, "That book is based more on reality than people know. It really is in there, and to me it is as close as you could come to what happened. This is the way it was." It is reality, but it is also myth on top of that. "Let the myth enter after the realism is made," Manfred said. "I like to go back to the Greeks. They had realism too. . . . In addition to realism we should get some sort of . . . well, I should say mental construction, get something into it that the higher reaches of our personality will be satisfied to look at" (C124). Thus, there are two basic levels of understanding to be enjoyed in reading *Riders of Judgment*—the historical or particular and the Grecian or universal.

In *Conversations*, Manfred says that the idea of writing about Nate Champion, the Wyoming range war hero, came to him while reading the *Banditti of the Plains* by Mercer, but that he did not know how to begin it or end it until he and his wife took a trip to Wyoming. They visited the state archives to look over Nate Champion material, and then they talked to friends and relatives of the range war heroes in Cheyenne, Casper, and Kaycee.

While visiting in Kaycee with Thelma Condit, a ranch wife and writer, the Manfreds were fortunate to be on hand when a carload of Tisdales, cousins of the Champions, came to visit Mrs. Condit. Johnny Tisdale was the oldest, a rodeo champion who was about to be born the day Nate Champion was killed. Nate was to have been his godfather. Manfred listened to their conversation all day and says, "I took as many notes as possible. So the conversation I have in *Riders of Judgment* is based a lot on this conversation I heard out there in Kaycee" (C122).

At one point during the writing, Manfred considered using the real name, Nate Champion, for his hero. He went so far as to write a preface, now in the University of Minnesota Archives, explaining that he used the historical name "because of what Nate did and because of what men have made of it." Manfred speculates in the discarded preface as to what Nate's reaction might have been to reading *Riders of Judgment:*

It's also possible Nate might admit that, in the deeper reaches of the thing, it probably went something like this (and if not like this then it could). He might not have been acquainted with the travails of an Orestes (just as Hamlet was not acquainted with those of an Oedipus) but he would know that in the soul of man "there is a lot of human cussedness and many a tarnal onnatural kink." Nate was a rider of judgment and as such knew his critters from cows on up.[32]

In a postscript to the preface, Manfred quotes an old "waddy" as telling him, "Why make up a new name for the man in your yarn when what his folks give him at birth, Nate Champion, happens to be perfect."[33]

But Manfred did make up a new name, Cain Hammett. As he explains in *Conversations*, he learned from his experience of using the real name Hugh Glass in *Lord Grizzly* that stories with historical names are not marketable. "All the Hollywood people wanted to do was buy the title from me and so get rid of me. Because, they said, they could go to history to get the story" (C125).

In spite of the fictitious names, readers of histories of the Johnson County War of 1892, such as Helena H. Smith's *War on Powder River*, will recognize that most of the characters have been based on real people and most of the events based on historical fact. A check of the histories will show that it is possible to identify twenty-three characters with some certainty. Of the main characters, only Rory and Gram seem to be purely fictional.

On top of the very real events and characters he has used in *Riders of Judgment*, Manfred has laid an aura of myth which ties these particular times and people to Greek and biblical heroes and stories. Even beyond these traditions, he has shown Cain to be inheritor of powerful animal forces from the deep past—forces which he struggles to control for good ends.

The use of Greek myth can be seen in several contexts. The Hammett family curse has correspondences with the curse on the House of Atreus; the fear of the eldest son that Gramp harbors is similar to the fear Cronus has of his son Zeus; and there is an Oedipal flavor in the competition between father and son.

From a biblical context, the sacrifice of the son by the father suggests Abraham and his command by God to sacrifice Isaac. As Hunt recalls his own near death as a boy at the hands of his father, his mind becomes a "whelming rage of hate, blixon hot. . . . God the father was an enemy."[34]

Other biblical contexts are suggested by the name "Cain Hammett." In Genesis, because Cain has slain his brother, he is made a "fugitive and a vagabond," asking: "Am I my brother's keeper?" Manfred's Cain, ironically, *is* his brother's keeper, even though he has killed unnecessarily. Harry, the rustler and secret plotter against his brother, is more akin to the biblical Cain.

Peter De Boer sees biblical implications also in the name "Hammett." Canaan, son of Ham, was given the following curse because he had seen his father's nakedness: "A servant of servants shall he be unto his brethren" (Genesis 9:25). Cain dies as a servant to the small cattlemen. De Boer points out the curious fact that if the biblical Canaan would have had a given name and a surname, it would have been Canaan Ham.[35]

There is a sound similarity in the two names, and for that matter, "Hammett" sounds not unlike "Hamlet." The quandary Cain is in over the need to kill Hunt Lawton in revenge for his father's death is similar to Hamlet's quandary. Like Hamlet, Cain ponders the eternal questions: "It was enough to make a man shiver and think on God, think even on the Devil, for that matter. Who was Cain Hammett? What was his horse?" (34). Rory's prodding is like Hamlet's ghost, pointing the need. There is something of the biblical Eve in her, too, as she teases Cain into violating what he knows instinctively to be right. The animal in him is betrayed, just as his horse Lonesome is sacrificed to the mission.

Cain expresses his quandary in biblical terms, too, seeing himself forsaken as Christ was:

My God, my God, why hast thou forsaken me? Why art thou so far from helping me, from the words of my rearing? But I am a worm, and no man. I am poured out like water. All my bones are out of joint. My heart is like wax. It is melted in the midst of my bowels. My strength is dried up like a potsherd. Thou has brought me into the dust of death. (227)

It is ironical that the horror prompting these thoughts—the hanging and mutilating of innocent Dencil Jager—is perpetrated not by Hunt, the enemy, but by friend Timberline and brother Harry.

It is in such ambiguous treatment of the good and the bad that *Riders of Judgment* is lifted above the level of a formula Western. It fits Cain's definition of "classic." As Hambone, Timberline, and Cain discuss their favorite songs, Cain says he likes the ballad "Riders of Judgment" best because it's classic: "Classic is when a song has got some judgment in it, and has got it in the best. Now you take 'Riders.' It's got heaven in it, and hell, and a lot of other tarnal matter. But better yet, it has got judgment in it" (322).

As a "Western" hero, Cain himself is hard to classify. He has the

"mark of Cain" and wears a black outfit rather than the white. He
has killed unnecessarily. Yet he holds fast to a strong sense of
morality. Peter De Boer lists the following good traits: (1) he throws
in with the little man, (2) he attacks Mitch and Cecil Guth for
berating Rory, (3) he is bothered because Avery Jimson will allow
his wife Queeny to entertain other men alone, (4) he believes in
winning through a fair fight, (5) he hates the way Timberline mistreats his horse, (6) he swears he will never kill again without good
reason, and (7) he has extraordinary cleanliness as a bachelor cowboy.[36]

Something of Cain's ambiguous nature is suggested early in the
book when Cain characterizes himself: "Here comes bachelor Cain
Hammett, he thought, a snowball in his left hand and a posey of
trueflowers in his right" (5). The same paradox can be seen in the
way others view Cain. Mitch calls him a "left handed saint" (138).
Harry says Rory had eyes only for Cain because inside he was
"granite along with a boiling heart" (160). When Cain was able to
bluff his way into the roundup camp, Harry senses that he has a
"lion inside" that is always under complete control.

The "lion inside" Cain is a figure that Manfred uses to tie *Riders
of Judgment* to traditions even older than the Greek or the
biblical—to the animal. Cain possesses this primeval power more
than any other character, though other Hammetts seem to have it as
well. It is the family "wild streak," which Harry cannot control but
which Cain is able to make work for good. When Cain's horse and
mule run from a snake, Cain "sent his voice out powerfully, letting
the animal in himself get into it, trying to make the animal in
himself stronger than the animal in Lonesome and the pack mule."
The animals stop, and Dencil is amazed, saying, "I've done some
strong things with horses that was a mystery too. But never the beat
of that" (27 - 28). But Cain does not want to go into why he could
control animals, why he could make his will their will. "He knew it
was somehow linked with his hot temper, the terrible temper he was
supposed to have inherited from Gramp Hammett. He knew the
less he thought about such things the better he was able to keep a
tight rein on himself" (28). Later Cain uses his animal power to save
his nephew Joey from the well. "Cain shot down his voice again,
this time powerfully low, letting the animal in him get into
it. . . ." Joey, "as if hypnotized," did it (63).

Cain's love for his black horse Lonesome is another expression of
his primal nature. His instincts tell him that he should not ride after

Hunt, but for the sake of Rory he does and kills Lonesome. Harry recognizes a similarity in the animal and the man. "You and that black horse are two of a kind and cancel each other out," he tells Cain. "You're both black devils" (40).

But Harry is the devil, the wild one. Cain asks him about his rustling. "Why do you do it, Harry?" Harry answers, "Once a wild one always a wild one." Cain counters, "To hell with that" (41). Cain accepts the responsibility for what he is. The resolution in Cain between the snow ball and the trueflower, between the animal and the human, is the resolution of the prehistoric and the aristocratic that occurs at the conclusion of the *Oresteia*. The conflicts of old are blended and reconciled. There is a fusion of opposites in the mean. Edith Hamilton writes of the Greek resolution in the person of Orestes: "Neither he nor any descendant of his would ever again be driven into evil by the irresistible power of the past. The curse of the House of Atreus was ended."[37]

When the end comes for Cain, he has the satisfaction of letting his power out for the good, "like a grizzly tormented into one desperate lunge and bite . . . all his life he'd had to hold his wild one in check for fear of going too far, of hurting someone. . . . Here now was a chance to let it out full force without having to worry about hurting the good" (341). As a rider of "judgment," Cain was ready for "that roundup of Ages . . . when the Riders of Judgment come down from the sky" (322).

But what of Cain's enemy, Hunt Lawton? In the *Oresteia*, the Furies are persuaded to accept the new law of mercy as a result of Orestes' acceptance of guilt for his actions. "I, not Apollo, was guilty of my mother's murder," Orestes said.[38] Cain, too, accepts blame for his own crimes, and the Reverend Creed preaching at Cain's funeral recognizes the guilt of the victors: "Now it stands for us to examine our own hearts. Some of us do not have clean hands" (367).

The Furies change from their frightful aspect and become the Eumenides, Benignant Ones. Hunt, however, seems unchanged even at the end, unless his response to the meadowlark can be seen as a sign. "That durn bird has been in my ear all day," he complains and takes a snap shot at it. He misses. The meadowlark soars off into the high dusk over the land (363). Similarly, as Cain's coffin is being lowered, a tiny wisp of steam spurts out of a crack into the cold air. "The puff rose and vanished against the clouds over the Big Stonies" (368).

Most critics have been kind to *Riders of Judgment*, praising it for its high seriousness, for authenticity and vivid sense impressions, and for its gripping narrative power.

On the other hand, Peter De Boer thinks *Riders of Judgment* is one of Manfred's weakest fictional works because Hunt's motivation as a killer is based on his memory of an attempted drowning when he was only two years old.[39] L. V. Jacks, in *Books on Trial* (June/July 1957), sees the book as a "muscular romance" with redundant dialogue and with too little attention paid to literary discipline.

A more favorable attitude is taken by Lewis Nordyke in the *New York Times Book Review* (5/26/57). He sees the action as sometimes gruesome, but having "the ring of fidelity to fact, a real thriller all the way." John R. Milton, in the *Cresset* for May 1958, liked the way Manfred let us smell and see the range: "*Riders of Judgment* is the living West. It is the next think to living through the experiences for one's self."

Joseph M. Flora sees *Riders of Judgment* as one of Manfred's major successes in joining plot and character and feels that his "ethical concerns make the novel something more than merely a historical novel. The novel, like all the Buckskin Man Tales, is a judgment on the American past and the American present."[40]

III   Conquering Horse *(1959)*

Even though Frederick Manfred's books fall naturally into certain categories, it would be a mistake to think that themes do not cross the categorical boundaries. One theme that does is his belief that the primal, animal instinct is of great value to human beings. In his inscription to the archives copy of *Conquering Horse*, Manfred calls attention to the way No Name learns about fatherhood by watching how the stallion Dancing Sun runs his band. He sees the stallion as a symbol for maleness and creativity. In *Milk of Wolves*, Manfred picks up this theme again, exploring it in greater detail as an artist faces both city and wilderness. The danger Manfred sees in the civilizing process is that the primal knowledge will be lost.

The Sioux brave, No Name, is a vehicle for Manfred's view in *Conquering Horse*. Denied a vision and therefore a name, he lacks honor as son of Chief Redbird. Without the vision, even though he is brave in battle, he cannot count coup or marry the virgin Leaf, whom he loves. Ironically, his dream sign, of a wild horse trying to kill him, comes after he takes Leaf's virginity and she vanishes. Moon Dreamer, his bachelor uncle and tribal medicine man, puts him through the purification rite and determines that his companion for the vision ordeal will be his rival, Circling Hawk. In the vision which comes after his ordeal atop the Butte of Thunders, No Name learns that he must capture a wild white stallion, but only after he tortures himself in the sun dance. He learns the second part of the vision after the dance, which is that he must kill his true father.

On his journey to the River That Sinks, he rescues Leaf, who has been buried to her neck in sand by the Pawnees and left to die. They travel into the Pawnee camp to learn from the friendly Pawnee, Sounds the Ground, the location of the white stallion. After patient stalking, No Name finally captures Dancing Sun, the horse of his vision, only to lose him as the animal leaps over a cliff in a thunderstorm and dies. Meanwhile Leaf, camped nearby, has given birth to a son; and Dancing Sun's mare has given birth to twins, one of which lives because Leaf nurses it.

The homecoming of Leaf and No Name is triumphant but sad, for No Name is committed to his vision and must kill Redbird. Redbird learns of the vision in a dream of his own and decides to die in the traditional way, by challenging the young braves to battle. At the last moment a storm comes up, and Redbird disappears in a flash of lightning.

Manfred's *Conquering Horse* holds a unique position among novels of the American Indian in that it does not depend upon cultural clash for its basic conflict. Indian life is seen as it existed just prior to the coming of the white man to Siouxland. In this cultural isolation, the Indian lifestyle, as interpreted by Manfred, has haunting reverberations from both Eastern and Western civilizations. Along with a structure and an atmosphere that resemble a classical Greek epic, *Conquering Horse* has a Whitmanesque link to Eastern mysticism.

The Grecian tone is struck, as D. E. Wylder has pointed out, through the epic pattern of events. Wylder sees Manfred's tale both as an *Odyssey* and an *Oedipus the King*. There is the Homeric focus upon the warrior hero, No Name, who in this instance is questing rather than returning; he is questing as an Oedipus for a relationship with his true father and for his true self.[41]

Conquering Horse has an epic spirit and most of the traditional characteristics of the epic as outlined in *A Handbook to Literature:*[42] (1) The hero is a figure of heroic stature—(No Name is son of a chief); (2) the setting is vast in scope (No Name travels to the far reaches of Siouxland, his known world); (3) the action consists of deeds of great valor (No Name conquers a fierce stallion through great courage and daring); (4) supernatural forces take an interest in the action and intervene (No Name relies on his vision and his "helper" for guidance in all that he does); (5) a style of sustained elevation and grand simplicity is used (Manfred invents a speech pattern for the Indians that reflects the rhythms of nature and suggests the nobility of primitive man). Manfred does not use other epic conventions, such as invoking the muses, beginning in the middle of things, making catalogues, or giving characters long formal speeches. However, he does give No Name a mysterious birth, typical of the mythic hero.

Redbird and his wife, Star, lose a son before No Name is born and are displeased because they cannot bring forth another child. Redbird tries and fails with three maidens. Then, miraculously, his first wife, Star, conceives. Because the white mare of No Name's vision chooses Moon Dreamer as intercessor for the sun dance, rather than Redbird, No Name begins to have doubts about his true father. Later we learn that Moon Dreamer, who remains a bachelor, had loved Star before Redbird took her. Other bits of evidence seem to indicate that Star has been impregnated by the medicine man, Moon Dreamer, who is also her brother. The incestuous possibility is often part of the mythic story line as well. Yet in the end it is Redbird who dies as the "true" father to complete the vision. The mystery holds.

Beyond its epic pattern, *Conquering Horse* carries a Grecian tone through echoes of ancient gods. Zeus, hurler of the thunderbolt, is suggested in Redbird, who has visited the Thunders and who returns to them mysteriously in a lightning flash. Eagles, spiders, and other living things give signs and help to No Name, much as the Greek gods helped their heroes.

Furthermore, the Cronus myth provides a controlling motif for the tale. Knowing that according to prophesy his sons will dethrone him, the Titan Cronus swallows his children as they are born. Their enraged mother, Rhea, hides her baby, Zeus, and tricks Cronus into swallowing a stone instead. Zeus grows to manhood and dethrones Cronus.

This universal competition between father and son, both of whom love and fear each other, is shown by Manfred to be operating on human and animal levels. No Name is shocked when the white mare of his vision, a Rhea or mother figure, tells him that his true father must die. "I love my father dearly. I cannot kill him," the anguished No Name tells Moon Dreamer.[43] No Name here assumes that he must be the instrument of death, whereas the vision says only that the true father must die.

No Name witnesses a fight to the death between Dancing Sun and Black One; then, later, as he is mourning for the dead Dancing Sun, he discovers under the scarlet mane a black streak. This shows him that Black One could well be the son of the white stallion. The parallel to his own dilemma haunts him later as he broods in worry about his return home to take over his father's band.

The mother-son relationship is explored as well in *Conquering Horse*. No Name watches as Dancing Sun kills a brown stud who stayed too long with his mother. No Name praises his mother, explaining to Leaf how she did not try to hold him back when he had to follow his dangerous vision.

In showing parallels between the animal and human worlds, Manfred reflects an Eastern mystical point of view. It is the view of Walt Whitman, who sees the universe as a single whole and man as kin to the plants, the animals, and the earth. Life is circular, he suggests in these lines from "Song of Myself": "I bequeath myself to the dirt to grow from the grass I love, / If you·want me again look for me under your boot-soles."[44]

After No Name weeps over the dead white stallion, crying, "I love you my brother. Why must you leave me?" he drinks the horse's blood and eats slices of his heart, saying:

"Horse, I give you to Wakantanka. I shall let you lie upon the rocks. I do this that the elements may take you back: the spirits your white coat, the air your lungs, the earth your blood, the rocks your bones, the worms your flesh. It was from all these that you were formed and it is to all these that you must return. Life is a circle. The power of the world works always in circles. All things try to be round. Life is all one. It begins in one place, it flows for all time, it returns to one place. The earth is all that lasts. I have said. Yelo." (287)

The experience with the horse helps him to reconcile himself to the confrontation with his father. Finally he gets nerve enough to visit Moon Dreamer, who helps him to receive the power of the white mare. Back in his tepee with Leaf, the meaning of his mystical experience comes to him:

He trembled with exultation. He quivered from head to foot. Little shivers stirred in the muscles all over and inside his body. He could still feel the power of the white mare throbbing in him. He now saw all life as one huge flow, with himself a streaming part of it. And being part of it he felt the whole of it. The huge flow included the lives of the wingeds and the four-leggeds and the two-leggeds, and also his life and the life of his father. One part of the flow was exactly like any other part of it. It was all one and the same. Therefore he no longer needed to think about how his father's life would end. (340 - 41)

In this effective blending of the ancient East and West with the native American Indian heritage, Manfred has achieved a masterpiece. He achieves it through a style that is at once elevated and simple, objective in the manner of the old Sioux herald Thunder Close By and yet omniscient enough to reveal the inner conflicts. To read *Conquering Horse* is to participate in a universal vision.

In reviewing the book for the *New York Times Book Review* (6/28/59), Paul Engle complained about some overly romantic moments, but he thought Manfred had "felt his way into a lively understanding of the Indian mind" and that it was a "fine and attractive story."

On the occasion of the reissue of the Buckskin Man Tales by New American Library/Signet, Madison Jones, writing in the *New York Times Book Review* (2/16/75), complimented Manfred on his narrative mastery through which "the most unpromising moments surprise us with their intensity." Jones cites the three day vigil of No Name as such a moment, "kept intensely alive through the hovering of insect or bird and charged with tension through intervals of cold, thirst and hunger." He says that the whole world is alive for Manfred, as it is for the Indians, which accounts for "the acuteness of his eye for detail and his gift for portraying the eloquence of purely sensual experience." Jones thinks that even greater than the historical value of *Conquering Horse* and the other tales is the "living breathing image of that part of Mother Earth that he has rendered for us with so much love and eloquence."

IV   Scarlet Plume *(1964)*

The concluding section of *Scarlet Plume* describes the hanging of thirty-eight Dakota (Sioux) Indians at Mankato, Minnesota, the day after Christmas in 1862. It remains the greatest single mass execution in the history of the United States. On the site of the hanging, a new library was completed in 1977, and efforts are being made to erect an appropriate memorial marker to the Sioux. The first memorial reconciliation ceremony, sponsored by the native Americans and the Mankato community, was held at the site November 5, 1975. A paragraph for a proposed marker reads as follows:

The Dakota War was a culmination of years of friction between Dakota and white as settlement pushed into Indian hunting grounds. Government agents and missionaries hoped the Dakota could be taught to live as farmers and worship as Christians, but, as Chief Big Eagle said many years later, "It seemed too sudden to make such a change. . . . If the Indians had tried to make the whites live like them, the whites would have resisted, and it was the same way with many Indians."[45]

However, in spite of public displays and political statements, even now there is not sufficient understanding among Indians and whites to settle the matter of an appropriate memorial. Not enough people have read *Scarlet Plume* and *Conquering Horse*. White students who read these tales in classes admit to having their eyes opened to a new appreciation for the culture and lifestyle of the Sioux. Because these fictions do get at universal truths and move people's hearts toward reconciliation, Manfred's books are to be cherished as instruments of peace.

In August of 1862, Judith Raveling, in *Scarlet Plume*, is visiting her missionary sister Theodosia at skywater, the present Lake Shetek in Minnesota, when Indians rise up in anger over treaty violations. Once Theodosia's husband Claude is shot, there is no stopping the massacre, in which all the men are killed and the women raped and tortured. Judith is captured and forced to serve as wife to Chief Whitebone of the Yankton tribe, which is relatively friendly to whites. She is given Indian clothes, participates in a buffalo drive, and learns Indian ways. She is attracted to Scarlet Plume, nephew to Whitebone, who tries to convince the chief that Judith should be returned to her people. While the men argue, Judith escapes and walks to the settlement at Sioux Falls, only to find it abandoned.

She starts the walk back toward St. Paul and is helped by Scarlet Plume, who has been following protectively all along. Judith seduces him, and they take the roles of husband and wife. Scarlet Plume hunts, protects her from Mad Bear, and they lead an idyllic life. It cannot last, however, for Scarlet Plume must follow his vision and return Judith to her people. When they get to Fort Ridgely, Colonel Sibley will not accept Judith's word that Scarlet Plume is innocent. As he is taken with the other prisoners to Mankato, the women of New Ulm attack and mutilate the bound Indians. Scarlet

Plume is hanged with thirty-seven other Sioux Indians the day after Christmas in Mankato. Judith rejects her true husband and heads west to be with the Yanktons.

Because *Scarlet Plume* represents the 1860s notch in the Buckskin Man Tales, its historical aspect is of initial interest, for the story is based on an event in the great Sioux uprising of 1862. However, in presenting this violent clash between two cultures, Manfred is as much interested in their similarities as in their differences, and he uses a love story to symbolize the common ground of our humanness. There is more in common, for example, between Scarlet Plume and Judith than between Judith and her husband Vince, who is ineffectual and unnatural. Thus, the historical aspect is somewhat taken over by a strong accent on the universal nature of love and love making. In fact, most of the contrasts between the two cultures are seen in terms of male-female or family relationships. An important factor in the leveling process is nature, in particular the virgin prairie, which reduces life to basics but is at the same time an idyllic setting for love. It is harsh yet beautiful. Manfred's story is both violent and romantic.

Something of Manfred's intent may be found in an early plan for *Scarlet Plume*, then titled *Heartland Fury*. He writes:

What is often forgotten is the fact that in Civil War days the standard of living for the Indian and white man was not so far apart as now. . . . In those days white men lived on dirt floors in sod huts, wore old clothes, were often lousy, didn't often take a bath, while the Indian lived in clean, often removed tepees, was kept in good leathers by his sewing wife, took baths often even in winter, and fought the lice. The better Indian males were much more attractive physically and spiritually, as proud men, than were the average whites. In fact it can be argued that such Indians as were noble were more noble than such whites as were noble. Many white women, coming from very poor families, were terribly drawn to the tall handsome red man. . . .[46]

A. Animals and Humans

A basic difference between white and Indian culture is in treatment of animals. Because the white man did not see himself as linked to all living things as a part of nature, he could treat the animal with contempt. The animal had no soul, as man did. The animal, in fact all of nature, was there for the white man's taking, as God intended. All he need do to justify the taking of Indian land and life was to declare the Indian animal.

Early in the book Silvers, the unscrupulous trader, says to Claude, the missionary, "Why, them red niggers desarve no better. They're hardly better than animals, in a manner of speakin' "[47]. At another point, Joe Utterback says, "Whoever thought the Indian had a soul must've surely lost his buttons" (43). Then Crydenwise agrees, "Ha. Ever try to domesticate a wolf? . . . A wolf'll snap at anything that comes near him even after he gets used to livin' with you. Same thing goes for a red devil" (43). In an early scene, Crydenwise has given a lesson on how the white man treats wolves and other animals. When Judith goes to warn him of the Indian attack, she finds him skinning a wolf alive and says to him:

> "But that's inhuman! Cruel. An awful thing to do."
> "What is?"
> "What you're doing. Why it's bestiality itself."
> "I know. I mean it to be." (13)

And it isn't just the animal that is skinned alive—the land is too. Joe Utterback says, "It haint' right fer an ignorant savage to own so much land, unplowed, while the better white man is forced to live in want. The Indian never did use the land for what the Lord intended it for—raisin' wheat" (27). This plowing of the land to the Indian is like raping the mother.

To be treated as Indians treat animals would be a mark of respect from the Indian viewpoint, for he considers animals his ancestors. All living things are related. Scarlet Plume tells Judith, "Even the grasses are related to us. They do not hesitate to feed on our fleshes after we die. . . . We are all one. We have a common mother. But the white man considers himself apart from this mother" (260). Just before the killing of the buffalo, Scarlet Plume prays: "This we do in memory of all the pa-pa who will die for us today. We are of their blood. We weep for them now because we already know their fate" (144). Then just before the first buffalo is skinned, Scarlet Plume says, "Friend, we thank you for letting us catch you. Friend, we too were animals before we were people, hence we must apologize now that we have killed you. Friend, we will not forget this. We thank you. I have said" (151). When the Indians then eat raw the parts of the animal that nourish like parts of man, Judith is sickened, while Scarlet Plume cannot understand her lack of religious feeling for the great gift of food.

The contrast of cultures is never more evident to Judith than when Scarlet Plume is ceremonially drinking the blood of a freshly killed deer. She feels "ice ages apart" from him and fears her "man-savage." Scarlet Plume tries to explain: "She the deer understands. The Yanktons were once animals before they were people. Her family and my family have been neighbors for many grandfathers. She and I are of one blood. Therefore the Yanktons are cousins to the deer and must apologize to her and thank her for the food and the doeskin" (258). Judith is confused and asks, "Does the Yankton consider the deer more of a brother than he does the white man?" Scarlet Plume explains:

In the beginning the red man welcomed the white man into his tepee. He considered him his kodah. He cried tears over him when he first met him. This was a great thing. But soon it could be seen that the white man wanted to cut up his mother into black strips and mutilate her. Our wise men saw that even as the red man gives when he has plenty, the white man takes when he has plenty. Does not the white man know that whatever one steals from his brother in this world he will have to carry it in the next world? Can he carry the world? The white man's thoughts are upside down. (258 - 59)

In this discussion over the killed deer, Judith comes to transfer to the Yankton tribe the sympathy she feels for the mother deer, for she sees that the Yanktons are to the white civilization as the deer are to the Yanktons. "Suppose this poor mother needed the blood of a Yankton? Your blood?" she asks.

"If it were fated to be, it would be for us to understand, a good thing," he answers (258). It is this fatalistic attitude that drives Scarlet Plume on toward the white encampment where he refuses to defend himself. As Judith watches the prisoners being taken to Mankato to be hanged, she thinks of Christ. "Scarlet Plume's iron control of his face reminded Judith of a Christ riding impassively to his fate, enduring chains and humiliations because a higher god expected it of him" (349). Scarlet Plume sees himself and his tribe sharing the fate of the deer and says, "Just as this mother deer is feeding us, so too the Yankton will be killed up and fed to the white man" (259).

B. *Giving and Taking*

Significant elements in the destruction of Indian culture are the greed and injustice that come along with such civilized though unnatural materials as coin and alcohol. The Yankton attitude toward gold is shown when Judith picks up a dandelion, thinking at first it might be a gold coin. "A good Yankton considers gold to be the dung of the gods. Goddung," Whitebone tells her (134).

The issue that finally triggers the massacre at Skywater is that of credit. The trader Silvers is doubly bad for the Indians, for he makes whisky for them and also serves as banker. Pounce, the supposedly Christianized Indian, says to Claude, "You take our money and give it to this trader . . . and he touches the pen to the books in a false manner and then says we owe it all to him" (49).

Whitebone senses that the greatest danger to his tribe is in their dependence on the white man's materials. In his speech reminding the Yanktons that they are the Center People of the Dakotas, he recounts how the old chiefs had forbidden the use of the white man's woolen blanket, pipe hat, silver spoons, and iron needles. He fears that He Who Has a Secret Name is angry because his people have kept iron guns and iron pots. He says, "When the white man gets mad he wants to kill everyone. There is no honor in it. It is just killing" (172).

It is killing for killing's sake and taking for taking's sake that the Yanktons cannot understand. Judith is stunned when, on the occasion of Smoky Day's death, Whitebone gives away not only all of Smoky Day's belongings but all of his own, because she was of his family (178). Judith recalls then how at the buffalo kill Whitebone went through the village to make sure that the poorest of the Yanktons had sufficient to eat. "Where does the red man come from," she cried aloud, "that he gives instead of takes?" She then realizes that the givers will be wiped out. "This is the very thing that will destroy you," she cries, and compares the Indian way of life to Christ's (179).

Judith finds it ironic that the white man took by force what he might have had through love; that without property or gold the Yanktons still had a profound sense of wealth; that with no records they still had a keen sense of history; that without clocks they nevertheless had a profound sense of time (267).

C. *Sex and Religion*

In contrast to the way in which Christianity tends to separate sex and religion, the Yanktons find a close relationship between the two. Typical of the attitude of the settlers is Judith's reaction to watching a cock and hen copulate. "The sight nauseated Judith. . . . Why didn't she peck him back a couple of times or two, to make him behave a little? . . . Cocky men burned Judith." Maggie Utterback expressed it another way: "You men are all a bunch of lazy good for nothin' boar pigs, the lot a ye."

In contrast to these attitudes, Manfred said that in writing *Scarlet Plume* he was trying to write about the masculine sweetness of life. "The male at his height," he says, "is like a stallion looking out over the herd."[48] Scarlet Plume is the "male at his height," and the way he secretly looks out for Judith on her trek to Sioux Falls is in the manner of the protective stallion. His demeanor is in stark contrast to the male examples among the settlers, who do little to protect their own. And it is in contrast to Judith's weak husband, who prefers unnatural sex. The implication is that the Indians learned rape from their white enemies. Raping to them is counting coup in the white manner. Under normal circumstances, the Indian expressed great reverence for women, and Judith herself is eventually treated as a white goddess. Whitebone explains the Yankton attitude: "The Shining People cannot be born from a foul place. They can only be born from a good place. And a good place is a sacred place. We worship all sacred things. . . . We worship the virgins. We cannot mistreat a sacred thing. The gods will punish us if we do. Thus it is that as long as our maidens remain virgins, the Buffalo Woman sends us much meat" (169 - 70).

With this sacred attitude toward the buffalo and the virgin, the buffalo dance becomes both a holy ceremony and a sexual performance, as Judith discovers when she secretly observes the naked dancers one evening. She sees that Scarlet Plume is aroused as he performs his role as a buffalo, and for the first time she feels drawn toward him as a man. "Judith couldn't help admitting it was more profoundly moving, more soul-rousing, than any Christian rite or ceremony she had ever witnessed in her life" (141).

In spite of all this male power, however, the Yanktons have a great fear of womankind. Menstruating women are kept in separation tents. When Judith sleeps with Whitebone during her period, he is so shocked that he faints (185). Tinkling, who had lived with a white man, explains to a bewildered Judith how the Yanktons feel: "Understand this. The Yanktons consider the woman spirit a powerful thing. If it is not kept in bonds it will destroy the man, perhaps even destroy the woman. When blood flows from that place where the child is born, it is a sign of the terrible power for harm in the woman. Therefore you must stay in the separation lodge until all danger is past" (185).

Judith doesn't quite know how to equate this attitude with her former opinions on equal rights for women. As she watches the members of Whitebone's tribe contentedly going about their daily chores, she is irked to see so many bowed-over women in camp. She finally says, "What a strange thing I see in the Yankton camp. The women do all the work while the men sit on their behinds doing nothing but eat and smoke and gossip" (119). Scarlet Plume is offended and explains why this is:

The men must hunt the meat, fight the enemy, steal the horses, and teach the boys. . . . The women must cook the meat, make the clothes, build the tepees, have the babies and feed them. . . . All this is just. And it can be seen that it is just when it is noted that the horses and the weapons and the honor feathers belong to the men, and the tepees and the parfleches and the food belong to the women. (119 - 20)

At this point in the story Judith has not fallen in love with Scarlet Plume and is truly appalled at the Yankton customs. That in a few more weeks she could accept them so fully has puzzled some readers. The romantic implication is that love makes all possible. In fact, one could see the book as focused sharply on this single theme of love, with the massacre, the culture shock, and the historical setting as mere complication designed to dramatize the power of sexual attraction between the red "male at his height" and the "white goddess." Love conquers all.

If the focus is thus concentrated on the power of love, the explicit details of love making contribute to the full documentation of this theme. There is evidence that Manfred intended it so, for the first line in his inscription on the flyleaf of the archives copy of *Scarlet Plume* is, "For me to live I must have love."[49] Virtually the same words are spoken by Judith after she and Scarlet Plume have had intercourse for the first time: "When I am not in love I am nothing" (266).

The love theme is sandwiched between red violence in the opening section and white violence in the closing episode. The human being, whether red or white, is shown to be capable of both love and violence. These contraries are two sides of the human coin. One closes *Scarlet Plume* with a feeling of sad regret that in our history the love side of the coin has not been "up" more often than the violent side.

Comments on *Scarlet Plume* at the time of its publication ranged from seeing it as a crude story which many will consider sheer trash, to finding in it a story with the depth of our common humanity. Negative criticism was focused on the shocking detail of the massacre and the explicitness of the sexual encounters, as well as on historical authenticity.

John K. Sherman in the *Minneapolis Tribune* (11/22/64) wrote: "Reading him is like listening to a modern day Homer, lyre in hand, relating and reliving old and sad and epic stories of our pre-beginnings when our land was wild and dangerous."

Roy W. Meyer, writing in *Minnesota History* (Spring 1965), would have liked more attention paid to causes, closer fidelity paid to events. He finds *Scarlet Plume* less authentic than *Conquering Horse* and regrets the emphasis on sex and violence at the expense of characterization and objectivity. In a similar vein, Victor P. Hass, in the *Chicago Tribune* (12/20/64), feels that the shocking preoccupation with sex serves to "cheapen his sometimes excellent presentation of the love of Judith and the god-like Scarlet Plume."

On the other hand, the *Chicago Daily News* (11/28/64) reviewer feels that the sexual passages were written with "such respect for sex that it is never demeaned," and that the story, with the naked strength of its prose, justifies itself.

The shocking facts of the massacre are taken detail for detail from written records of survivors of the Lake Shetek tragedy, to be seen in the Minnesota Historical Society Archives. The basic circumstance of the story, that of a white woman in love with an Indian fated to hang, is recorded in a letter of Colonel Sibley to his wife, used by Manfred as his frontispiece. Reviewer John K. Sherman feels that Manfred was able to lead away successfully from the violence of the opening sections and that the reader through *Scarlet Plume* encounters history in the human terms of tears and grief, calamity and ecstasy.

V   King of Spades *(1966)*

As the concluding tale of the Buckskin Man Tales, *King of Spades* carries echoes of all the others. Earl Ransom's coming of age is in tragic contrast to No Name's heroic transformation in *Conquering*

Horse; the winter in Eden that Ransom has with Blue Swallow recalls the Edens Hugh Glass experiences with his Bending Reed; the Ransom-Erden love episode replays the Scarlet Plume-Judith affair, with the roles reversed, but ending with a hanging; the incest theme in *Riders of Judgment* is intensified in *King of Spades*, as the sex relationship moves from first cousins to mother and son.

In spite of these echoes, *King of Spades* is not like any of the other Buckskin Man Tales. It defies categorization, according to Brian Garfield in the *Saturday Review* (10/22/66), who finds it the tallest of tall tales, fascinating for its tongue-in-cheek unbelievability. He writes: "*King of Spades* is a spectacular fable, a black comedy, a pop tragedy, or—have it as you will—an upright, downright, folk-mythic Western. . . . It is compounded of equal parts of Alfred Henry Lewis's Wolfville Tales, *Oedipus Rex*, grade Z Western, period costume melodrama, and Pecos Bill."

Son of aristocratic English parents who lose their wealth in Siouxland, Magnus King upon their death attends medical school in Chicago and marries his landlady's thirteen year old daughter Katherine (Kitty). The new doctor takes his young bride to the frontier town of Sioux City, Iowa, where he sets up practice. Their son Roddy grows up with an unnatural attraction for his mother, and this makes Magnus so insanely jealous that he shoots Kitty through an eye, only to be shot in turn by Roddy, who then runs away.

The scene shifts to Wyoming, where a young cowboy, Earl Ransom, and an old salt, Sam Slaymaker, pay a visit to the Stinging Lizard brothel, run by Kate, a handsome madam with a patch over one eye. In a brawl over cards, a muleskinner shoots Sam, and Ransom shoots the muleskinner. Kate saves Ransom from the law by pretending to be married to him, and they set up housekeeping. However, Ransom leaves for the Black Hills when gold is found there.

He spends an idyllic winter in the forest with Erden Aldridge (Blue Swallow), a white girl Indian-reared, but greedy miners intrude on their paradise; and Erden leaves, pregnant with Ransom's child. Ransom is caught up in gold fever, becomes wealthy, helps found the town of Deadwood. Kate joins him, but Ransom, having known Erden, is no longer satisfied with Kate. He grows sullen, kills two men in bar brawls, and finally shoots Kate. As Ransom is being tried, his father, Magnus King, arrives and recognizes Ransom as Roddy and the dead Kate as his wife Kitty. On the gallows, overwhelmed with the knowledge that he has slept with and killed his mother, Ransom kicks himself free and drops to his death.

King of Spades may be hard to classify, but it has three well-defined themes. There is a "nationhood" theme, common to all the Buckskin Tales, which in *King of Spades* is focused on the relationship between aristocracy and democracy, the turning of one into the other in the American West. On top of this, Manfred deliberately overlays the Oedipus myth—his own interpretation of it from the point of view of the father. The imagery of the myth is preparation for the "ecological" theme related to the violation of Eden, the corruption of nature by the civilized greed for gold and possessions.

A. Nationhood

By using the name "King" for his leading characters, Manfred immediately sets up a contrast between the old world of kings and the new one of individualists on the frontier. Magnus King's first memories are of his father fixing a monocle in his eye and telling about the illustrious kings back in the old country.[50] When little Magnus fights for his rights, his mother compliments him, saying, "Now you begin to sound like my father, your grandfather the earl. A true king after all" (7). The influence of the old aristocracy is symbolized throughout the book with the monocle image. When Roddy asks his father when he can have a monocle, Magnus says, "Never. . . . It doesn't fit in America" (41). Ransom, the mature Roddy, does, however, have a habit of touching his eye and cheek as if he were adjusting a monocle. It is a gesture that helps Magnus identify him as Roddy. The monocle habit is associated with the killing habit, which spells doom for Ransom. Magnus has taught him well to take a life for a life, an Old Testament and old world notion. "The root of this new world tragedy," Russell Roth points out, "is in the old: in the English way of life that . . . prompts Magnus King to commit the senseless act that puts the ancient Oedipus myth in motion."[51] Roth sees Ransom's tragic end as an example of the inability of the pioneer to free himself from aristocratic ways, to slough off the old skin for new.[52] Faced with a choice, Erden or gold, Ransom chooses gold. On the scaffold he sobs, "And I betrayed her. For what? For money. For gold" (301).

B. Oedipus

While the nationhood theme is important as a link to the other four Buckskin Tales, quite clearly the Oedipus myth dominated Manfred's thinking as he prepared to write *King of Spades*. In a note titled "General Description of Current Plan," he sees himself telling the Oedipus story over again except that he wants to see what the father might think. In an interview before the writing of *King of Spades*, Manfred told John Milton that he planned to "go after" the father theme in his next book because it had been neglected in favor of the mother-son problem. He explained that, whereas a woman naturally loves her children, the man has to learn to be a father (C62).

Magnus King certainly had to learn the hard way about fatherhood. The jealousy he feels toward his son is insane, but there is provocation in the unnaturally strong relationship that develops between Kitty and Roddy. Kitty allows the roles of father and son to be reversed in what appears to be an innocent way. After all, she is very young, an early teenager. When Magnus comes home to find Roddy in his bed beside Kitty, he shouts, "What the hell is my son doing in my bed?" To which Kitty replies, "Roddy's had a hard day, shh, don't wake him" (33). Unwilling to face the prospect of a son as sexual competitor, Magnus creates the fiction that Kitty has a lover. He then trains Roddy to protect her if she is attacked, even by her husband. In the concluding scene, Magnus, now sane, wants to tell his son of his guilt, wants to take his son's place as the responsible party to the deed:

But, oh! I so wanted to tell him that it was me who did the wrong, not he. That I was the jealous one, of my wife's love for him and of his love for her. As so often happens between father and son and mother. When a son gets over into a father's territory, you know, sits in his armchair at the head of the table sometimes, there's bound to be a clash someday. (292)

The fatherhood of Magnus is set against the surrogate fatherhood of Sam Slaymaker. When Roddy emerges in the West as Ransom, memory lost, Sam teaches him the ways of the West and tries to initiate him into the ways of sex at Kate's Stinging Lizard brothel. Ironically, Sam would like to marry Kate, Ransom's mother, but Kate is not willing. Thus the possibility of a second competition between a father and son over Kate is in the mix, but Horses intervenes and Sam is shot.

Manfred ends the book with an enigmatic question: "When a son's blood is finally spilled, which mother weeps most? The stallions" (304). There is here the paradox of father as mother, perhaps an extension of the notion of Adam as mother to Eve. That the stallions weep most may be because of the jealousy they must fight to achieve their love.

C. *Ecology*

The love making between Kate and Ransom not only carries on the parallel to the Oedipus myth, but also sets up the symbolism associated with the ecological theme. Ransom's rape of his mother, his killing of her, is equivalent to the rape of mother earth for gold at Deadwood gulch, with the miner's spade as phallus and Ransom as King of Spades. It is a role he didn't ask for. His instincts and his dreams warn him away from Kate, and he wants to save himself for his perfect mate, but his gun and his father's training set up the circumstance which puts him in Kate's arms.

He has a second chance with Erden, his dream partner. As they come to each other, Ransom regrets that it wouldn't be the first time for him, while it would be for her: "A wandering Adam for a wilderness Eve. With gold as their Devil in Eden" (159). Gold is a devil that tarnishes even the perfect natural love between Ransom and Erden. During the very act of initial conquest of the Wild Girl, Ransom's mind is on gold: "It was crazy to think the Army might be able to keep the white man out of the Black Hills. Where gold, money, was involved the white man was worse than a hog. As even he himself was" (161).

Erden recognizes gold as her rival and tries to keep Ransom from prospecting, but he sees himself as the richest man in the world. He senses the impossibility of stopping the rush for gold and wants his cut. When he dreams of a future life with Erden, it is in town in a fancy brick house, not in the wilderness. Both Erden and Ransom are victims of forces and changes beyond their control. Eden is denied them, is turned into hell: "Deadwood resembled a new prairie-dog town. What had once been a lovely dell was now suddenly a dusty hell of uprooted earth" (209).

This contrast between Eden and hell is maintained throughout the final scene, as swallows dart and swoop around the men conducting Ransom's trial. They remind us of Erden, whose Indian name is Blue Swallow, and of her natural innocence, in contrast with the lust that has made the trial necessary and has brought civilization to Deadwood.

To open the Buckskin Man Tales, Manfred uses a D. H. Lawrence quotation which calls for the placating of the demons of

America, an atoning for the Spirit of Place. To close the series, he might have selected another Lawrence paragraph from the same essay:

The white man's mind and soul are divided between these two things: Innocence and lust, the Spirit and Sensuality. Sensuality always carries a stigma, and is therefore more deeply desired, or lusted after. But spirituality alone gives the sense of uplift, exaltation, and "winged life," with the inevitable reaction into sin and spite. So the white man is divided against himself. He plays off one side of himself against the other side, till it is really a tale told by an idiot, and nauseating.[53]

In Ransom, this division of self has resulted in a "nauseating" tragedy, over which the swallows, "winged life," play just out of reach.

King of Spades attracted extreme positions from reviewers. Victor P. Hass of the *Chicago Tribune* (11/20/66) write, "It has been a long time since I have read a novel as distasteful, absurdly violent , and luridly melodramatic." The reviewer for *The Omaha World Herald* (11/6/66) objected to the explicit love making scenes which, he says, had the capacity to shock thirty years ago but which today are employed mainly by hacks "who write to titillate the yahoos."

On the other hand, E. C. Kiessling, in *The Milwaukee Journal* (12/25/66), wrote that one scarcely notices the "implausibility of the plot in the intensity and excitement of the story." Jack Conroy, in the *Chicago Daily News* (10/29/66), thought "Manfred's narrative power . . . was never displayed to greater advantage."

Several reviewers felt that, in addition to being a good "story as story," it broke new ground in Western writing. In a letter to Trident Press, Herbert Krause, the novelist, wrote, "The book will shake the vitals of any reader who accepts the traditional picture of Deadwood and the gold field. Never before has this region been portrayed as it is in this rambunctious pistol jetting novel."[54] David W. Read, in the *St. Louis Post Dispatch* (3/12/67), found *King of Spades* to be a "powerful outpouring of one man's vision of the violence behind the smiling righteousness that satisfied so many readers of *The Virginian*. As such *King of Spades* is very much for our times."

VI   The Manly-Hearted Woman (1976)

Though *King of Spades* in 1966 was written as the concluding Buckskin Man Tale, Manfred returned to the subject and time a decade later. *The Manly-Hearted Woman* can be regarded as another tale, a bonus to his original plan.

The hero this time is Flat Warclub, a Yankton Sioux, who has a vision more womanly than manly. He sees how to help his tribe find clams in a stream, and because he wears a clamshell in his hair, he is shunned and not respected as a warrior. His band, the People of the Talking Water, are asked to help the Blue Mounds band fight the Omahas, who are threatening to take the Blue Mounds buffalo jump as their own. Flat Warclub is told by his "helper" to join the war party as it visits the Blue Mounds camp and prepares for battle.

The other braves quickly find hosts, but Flat Warclub is ignored by all except Manly Heart, who is a woman playing the role of a brave. She has taken Pretty Head as wife after two unsuccessful marriages to men. Because she has had a manly vision and has been successful hunting buffalo, the Blue Mounds people have accepted her male role as "wakan" or of the gods. In a fainting vision, Flat Warclub sees that he is fated to die in the coming battle, after killing seven of the enemy. Having convinced the leaders that he is fated to bring them victory, he becomes a hero and is granted freedom to have intercourse with any of the women he chooses. He mates with seven, including Pretty Head, but refuses to mate with Manly Heart, who has come to desire him. The battle goes as Flat Warclub had predicted, and he is killed. After his death, Manly Heart's male characteristics disappear, and she lives the rest of her years in silence.

Although Manfred's two most recently published novels appear to be widely different in theme, setting, and time, there is an interesting parallel to be drawn between *Milk of Wolves* and *The Manly-Hearted Woman*. Both explore the role of the "outsider" in society, whether he be excluded for sexual deviation, for mystical insight, or for creative talent. Such an individualist is often ridiculed by his contemporaries, only to be glorified later for his service to the group. Closely associated with this theme is the connection of the supernatural to the isolated one and the "intimations of immortality" that are associated with the person who is unique.

A. *The Outsider*

Both Flat Warclub and Manly Heart are rejected at first by their peers for deviant behavior, though both are able to experience "normal" sexual desires. Having had a "woman's" vision in locating clams for his band, Flat Warclub wears a clamshell in his hair and is

shunned by other braves as an inadequate male. However, he has
had a legitimate vision, and his helper encourages him to join the
war party against the Omahas, even though death is seen as a consequence. When Flat Warclub arrives at the sister band's camp, he
is humiliated because no family invites him as guest, until at last
Manly Heart does. The two outsiders share their separateness.
Following the advice of his helper, Flat Warclub continues to
behave in a singular manner. He has himself carried late into the
warrior dinner on a buffalo robe and is reprimanded by Chief Seven
Sticks, who says, "But do you not know that the good of the band is
always more highly valued than the good of the single soul?" Flat
Warclub counters the chief, however, saying, "For this one time it
is fated that the road taken by this single soul will be the salvation
of the whole"[55]. Furthermore, Flat Warclub is critical of the group:

You speak of me as behaving in a singular manner. Am I alone in this? Was
it not strange that the people of the Blue Mounds should let me sit alone on
my horse in their midst after we first arrived? Only the little children had
time for me with their sweet innocent wonderment. Where was the famed
good heart of the Dakota at that moment? Ee-ka. I wonder. . . . And was
it not strange that it was one of your strange braves to be the only one to
welcome this soul to camp lodge? (75)

Flat Warclub's plea is for tolerance of the unique person among
them. The words of America's celebrated outsider, Walt Whitman,
are appropriate in this context:

This is the meal equally set, this the meat for natural hunger,
It is for the wicked just the same as the righteous, I make appointments
with all,
I will not have a single person slighted or left away,
The kept-woman, sponger, thief, are hereby invited,
The heavy-lipp'd slave is invited, the venerealee is invited;
There shall be no difference between them and the rest.[56]

B. *The Supernatural Helper*

Once the Indians get some sign of approval from the spirit world,
the deviant person is accepted and even honored. Flat Warclub is
tolerated in his eccentricities when he can show that his helper is
telling him what to do; and Manly Heart is fully accepted as a
hunter once she has her eagle vision and the aid of her helper. She
is then bold enough to ask for Pretty Head as a bride, trusting that

her helper will show her how to behave in this unusual circumstance. When Manly Heart's menstrual periods end, her neighbors are convinced that her behavior is "wakan," approved by the gods, and she is accepted. After Flat Warclub has made love to Pretty Head, so that a child may come to the barren tepee, she feels "struck by lightning," where "girl play" only provided a friction spark by comparison. Flat Warclub is puzzled by it all: "He could not get a clear picture of what she meant by girl play. Yet whatever it was it had to be a good thing; otherwise the gods would not have permitted it" (161). There is a sense that whatever is, is good. Even the unattractive and sour Bitten Nose is tolerated by the band; and Flat Warclub, who overhears him in prayer, feels compassion toward him and sees his importance in the fated pattern of life.

In fact, the more peculiar the behavior, the more likely the deviant person is to be seen as wakan. In their treatment of Flat Warclub, the Blue Mounds band demonstrate both pagan and Christian characteristics in an archetypal ritual. Gradually the people come to see Flat Warclub as a savior, a god who has come to dwell among them for a time. Not only will he give up his life for them, but he will sow his seed on many so that he will be resurrected in his children to always dwell among them. He has his Judas in Bitten Nose.

These Christian overtones are blended with a pagan Saturnalia ritual, as Flat Warclub is given license to make love to any woman in the band. This ancient festival fell in December and was popularly supposed to commemorate the merry reign of Saturn, god of growing and husbandry. Feasting, revelry, and mad pursuit of pleasure were features that marked the carnival, which went on for seven days. An outstanding feature was the license granted slaves, who were allowed to replace their masters for a time, much as the lowly outcast Flat Warclub becomes the leader of the war party. However, a darker aspect of the Saturnalia has been discovered as it was practiced by Roman soldiers stationed on the Danube in the reign of Maximian and Diocletian. The following account appears in Frazer's *The New Golden Bough*:

Thirty days before the festival they chose by lot from amongst themselves a young and handsome man, who was then clothed in royal attire to resemble Saturn. Thus arrayed and attended by a multitude of soldiers he went about in public with full license to indulge his passions and to taste every pleasure, however base and shameful. But if his reign was merry, it was short and ended tragically; for when the thirty days were up and the

festival of Saturn had come, he cut his own throat on the altar of the god
whom he personated.[57]

Instead of killing the mock king, later celebrants merely appointed
him to rule over the festivities. In whatever form, the Saturnalia
dramatizes the role of the good god who gave his life for the world.

As a representative of that "good god," Flat Warclub discovers
sex and enjoys it so much that he wonders if he should welcome his
death so easily. His helper says to him: "Listen. The gods are giving
you a few extra bones to suck to make up for throwing your life
away. In ordinary life they would not have been given to you even
scattered over many years. Thus be happy. All is well. You shall live
a very juicy life in the next few days" (87). What his helper says is
true, and in fulfilling the prophecy, Flat Warclub's ordeal is a
mystical recognition of life as never ending or circular. This feeling
is enhanced by the way the magical number seven is associated with
his vision. He sleeps with seven women and then kills seven of the
enemy before he is himself killed by Bitten Nose. The chief's name
is Seven Sticks, from the number of sticks he always uses to start a
fire. Before the pipe is smoked, it is held to the seven directions:
north, south, east, west, heaven, earth, and the center.

The number seven is symbolic of perfect order, a complete period
or cycle. It comprises the union of the ternary and the quaternary,
as in the reconciliation of the square with the triangle, or sky over
earth. It is the number forming the basic series of musical notes,
colors, and of the planetary spheres.[58]

Chief Seven Sticks at first sees Flat Warclub as breaking the
magic circle so important to Indian well-being. He reminds Flat
Warclub, who grew up without a father, of the most important
lesson all fathers teach their sons—to follow their leader in all
things. The chief says:

This was done that I might make of my life here on these wide plains, to
the uttermost, an unbroken circle, of circles within circles, of family, of
band, of tribe, of nation. For the circle is wakan. That is why our tepees are
built in a circle. That is why our encampments are always set in a circle. A
wiser and better rule of life no man has ever discovered, nor ever will, nor a
truer art of victory or of happiness. . . . We have all been taught, even
from the very cradleboard, to think first of our neighbor and last of our belly. (73)

Although Flat Warclub had seemed to be selfishly drawing attention to himself, his singular behavior is in the best interest of the band. He will be their savior, and in sowing his seed, he will return to them after death through his children. As Flat Warclub is dying, "Suddenly he saw his life coming full circle. In a moment he would start the circle a second time around. The circle always brought the sun, and the sun always brought life and power. It was going to be doubly sweet the second time."

Here again Manfred shows a parallel between Indian belief and the philosophy of Walt Whitman, who wrote:

What do you think has become of the young and old men?
And what do you think has become of the women and children?

They are alive and well somewhere,
The smallest sprout shows there is really no death,
And if ever there was it led forward life, and does not wait at the end to arrest it,
And ceas'd the moment life appear'd.

All goes onward and outward, nothing collapses,
And to die is different from what any one supposed, and luckier.[59]

Manly Heart is given a glimpse of that "somewhere" as she questions her helper. She is amazed to learn that her helper knows Flat Warclub's helper. "They have lives in the other world, yes," her helper says. When Manly Heart asks, "Are they also born? Do they die?" the helper is not so direct:

"Those are old questions asked as a child might ask them. We stand ready behind the sun at all times, and when a young man receives his vision on a high place we quickly enter his chosen fetish and become his guardian spirit. Even as we did at last with you. And we remain in his fetish until it is fated that he dies. After that we return to our old places behind the sun and wait for the next call to earth." (110)

"There is then another world behind us," Flat Warclub says upon hearing that the two helpers communicate. "Ae, and it is also ahead of us," he is told (111).

The Manly-Hearted Woman is listed as a novel by Manfred and not as one of the tales, but it makes a good companion piece for *Conquering Horse*. The two together become a sociological study of primitive community life and a kind of bible explaining the mystical religion practiced by the Plains Indians.

Reviewers have been impressed with Manfred's ability to suggest through his use of language the rhythms and tone of another people in another time. In *America* (11/13/76), the reviewer says, "Whether or not Indians ever talked this way, Manfred's inner and outer dialogues are beautifully imagistic; his knowledge of Indian culture seems deep." James R. Frakes, in the *New York Times Book Review* (5/23/76), thinks the novel reads like a literal translation, both strange and haunting. He likes Manfred's word innovations, such as "swalving," "quirked," "clittered," and "eenked." Delbert Wylder sees *The Manly-Hearted Woman* as Manfred's most artistically perfect novel, of such complexity that critics will be kept busy for years.[60]

CHAPTER 4

Reminiscing and Romancing in Mid-America: Rumes, Romances, Stories, and Poems

IN a postscript to *The Giant*, titled "A Modest Proposal Concerning the 'Rume,'" Manfred explains in some detail how he came to coin the word "rume." When his second book, *Boy Almighty*, was ready for publication in 1945, he felt that it was somehow different from *The Golden Bowl*, and he did not want to call it a novel: "*Boy* was a personal and a vital truth, a testament of suffering and of faith in life, a tale with roots that went back to my private inner life, an odyssey created out of my very flesh and blood, as if the words were my cells and the phrases my tissues and the paragraphs my organs and the book my body"[1]. His publisher insisted on calling the book a novel, even so, but when Manfred came to write *Wanderlust* in the *Boy Almighty* manner, he began to search seriously for a better word to describe what he was doing. After considering long lists of possible words, he settled upon "rume," derived from such words as "rune," "rumor," "ruminate," and the Aryan word "RU," to sound, cry out, bray, yell.

The rume. After deep rumination, after long inner musing, a man cries out, "RU-es," "rhues" forth among men that thus and so has he felt about living. "I was here," he cries, "and I had this happen to me, and this I did, and these things I saw and discovered, and this is what I think it all means in these times and in this place on this earth in this galaxy in this universe.[2]

Manfred sees the rume as an autobiographical form made universal by exalting and transmuting personal agonies. It is a passionate avowal where the novel is an objective statement. According to this definition, then, *Boy Almighty*, *Wanderlust*, and *Green Earth* may properly be called rumes.

I   Boy Almighty (1945)

In April of 1940, Manfred entered the Glen Lake Tuberculosis Sanitorium, Oak Terrace, Minnesota. He thinks he may have picked up the germ back in 1936 when he was working in Sioux Falls and that the disease finally struck him down after he had weakened himself with too little food and too much smoking while working on his first novel.

Eric Frey's battle with tuberculosis is similar to that waged by Manfred between 1940 and 1942. Eric, a struggling writer, has Manfred's physique but not altogether his personality. Eric collapses in his rented room in the Twin Cities and is taken to the Phoenix Sanatorium, where he fights for his life against the disease. He visualizes his consciousness as the flickering of a flame and the pain as the gnawing of an animal inside him. As he settles into the sanatorium routine, he thinks over his past life and associates his father with "The Whipper," whatever force it is in the universe that is out to get him. When his father visits and brings a gift of handmade slippers, a reconcilliation of sorts is made, but Eric rejects the local dominie. Nevertheless, Eric's spiritual self is under treatment as well as his body. He learns about discipline from the kindly Dr. Abraham; about humility and courage from his roommates, Dr. Fawkes and Huck Olson; and how to resist temptation from the cynical Wybren Deeble. From another patient, Mary Lehar, he learns love. They date as best they can under the strict rules and plan to marry. Both Olson and Fawkes die, but Eric survives, having learned from them that the Whipper can be beaten since it is a force within the individual. He now accepts both the blame and the responsibility for his life.

At a question and answer session following one of Manfred's lectures, a student asked, "What is the source of your creative power?" "The sun," Manfred answered.

In Boy Almighty, there are a number of sun and flame images, which Manfred associates with health, life, physical energy, and power. Eric Frey's life is hanging in the balance when he is brought to the Phoenix Sanatorium, the name itself suggesting new life from flames. On a bad morning, he asks the nurse to roll him where he can see the sun, but she can't. On another morning, Eric is surprised to find the brightest sunshine he has ever seen. "But he wanted to leap about. He was sure that he could dance again. It was ennobling, this sunshine. It was a gift he had never expected to get again"[3].

In another passage Manfred reveals a mystical feeling of brotherhood toward the sun which might easily fit into one of his Indian books:

He tried to imagine what it would be like to have the sun come up on the eastern horizon, fresh and beaming and ennobling, coming upon the world, and he not there to welcome it with his flame. It could not be! Were he to go tonight, there would be clouds in the morning. There would be clouds. The universe would sorrow for him. The spheres of heaven would wail. The moon would weep inconsolably for him. The sun would warm the world in vain. (34)

Thus, the sun is personalized and becomes a "helper" to Eric. "I crave sunlight. I'm a sunshine boy," he tells Mary (253).

In contrast to this "good" outside force, Eric must deal with what he imagines to be a malign influence over him, which he calls the "Whipper." " 'Sometimes I think there's a devil out to do me dirt,' he tells his nurse, only in the next breath to contradict himself, saying, 'But that's foolish. Such talk only helps to dig the grave deeper' " (38). Eric's attitude toward the Whipper is ambiguous. He wants to accuse something or someone of making him ill, but he knows that such accusation is not justified. When the dominie from his home church suggests that a Holy God is chastising him for some sin, he grows angry: "What were they trying to say, that he was here because a God, a father, a whipper, was punishing him?" (44). Yet later, when Fawkes questions him, he is embarrassed about his belief in a Whipper and explains that it is "something in the universe, a hard hearted God" (102).

It is Fawkes who helps resolve for Eric the problem of the Whipper. Just as Dr. Abraham guides him to physical health by teaching him self-discipline, so Dr. Fawkes guides him to spiritual health by showing him that the Whipper can be beaten. In mourning Fawkes' death, Eric thinks: "I loved you because you taught me that the Whipper does not exist except in ourselves, and that we find order or chaos just as we choose. I loved you because you opened a door for me, because you taught me to use myself as a pivot from which to strike for life" (275).

Dr. Abraham, too, shows Eric that his helper as well as his enemy is within. He asks him to control his impetuous nature and to take each day as it comes. "My boy, a man may have the passion of a stallion, but until he's learned to discipline it, he can never hope to become a lover, an artist" (239).

Eric shows that he has learned discipline by pacing himself as he walks up the hill; then, after watching the stallion make love, he demonstrates discipline in controlling his passion when he could have imitated the stallion with Mary. In recognizing his own inner strength, Eric has come quite a way from the early days of his confinement when he looked to the sun for help and blamed the Whipper, a force outside himself, for his misfortune. Fawkes, the scientist, shows Eric that he cannot be a target for some universal power: "You see, the true Whipper is neither concerned nor unconcerned about us. He is a universe that has no knowledge of us. He can't have. Because he neither feels, nor hears, nor sees . . . nor probably knows" (264). Eric's spiritual journey is not unlike that of Job, who suffers boils and misfortunes even though he is righteous. Why? Job's supposed comforters are sure it is because he has done something wrong. Have not all these disasters taken place? God is a righteous God, and he does not punish without reason, they explain. Zophar says: "Oh that God would speak, and open his lips against thee, and that he would show thee the secrets of wisdom, that they are double to that which is! Know therefore that God exacteth of thee less than thine iniquity deserveth." (Job 11:5 - 6) And to Eric, Dominie Donner says:

"Eric, if you, poor humble sinner that you are, don't recognize that you are a sinner, if you don't go to the Lord on your hands and knees to beg Him for forgiveness . . . why! I warn you, it'll not go well with your soul." (42)
"God doesn't punish people with consumption unless he has something in mind. . . . That consumption that God gave you has a meaning. He's trying to tell you something." (43)

Both Eric and Job express anger at such admonitions. The dominie is sent from Eric's room, and Job says to Zophar: "No doubt but ye are the people, and wisdom shall die with you. But I have understanding as well as you; I am not inferior to you; yea, who knoweth not such things as these?" (Job 12:2 - 3).

Job trusts God, but has sufficient dignity to attest his own virtue and to hold ideas that are as horrifying to his platitudinous friends as Eric's ideas are horrifying to Dominie Donner. Job does not understand God's inscrutable justice, and he admits that he may have had secret faults, but these were his own and not to be revealed in public. He will not submit to the judgment of his friends, the popular judgment on disaster, but says, "My righteousness I hold fast, and will not let it go: my heart shall not reproach me so long as I live" (Job 27:5 - 6).

Job's "inner awareness" of his own integrity is the attitude of mind both Dr. Abraham and Dr. Fawkes try to instill in Eric. He need not bow down to the traditions of his past nor blame his misfortune on any "outside" force. That force is unconcerned.

There are biblical echoes as well in Manfred's use of the names Martha and Mary. In reflecting on the arrogance of Martha and the humility of Mary, Eric thinks that Jesus must have noticed somewhat the same difference in the Martha and Mary of his day. Such "doubling" of characters is a literary device Manfred employs most significantly in *Morning Red*. In *Boy Almighty*, he matches a number of characters along the division represented by the biblical Martha and Mary. That division is one basic to human personality. Alan Watts says that these two types may be named the "prickly" people and the "gooey" people. The pricklies, he says, the Marthas, are tough-minded, rigorous, and precise and like to stress differences and divisions between things. The gooeys, the Marys, are tender-minded romanticists who love wide generalizations and grand syntheses.[4]

As Eric becomes aware of his surroundings in the sanatorium, one of his nurses, Miss Berg, reminds him of his mother, a Mary type; and another, Miss Pulvermacher, reminds him of his father and Martha. "She had the cold hostile eyes of a Martha! of Pa!" (30). Similarly, where he sees his roommate Huck Olson as an inscrutable Martha, he sees his other roommate, Hawkes, as a warm Mary figure. From Eric's standpoint, the Marys are the helpers and the Marthas are the punishers, so that Pa and Martha and Nurse Pulvermacher are often associated with the Whipper and are blamed for Eric's plight. In fact, Eric's attitude toward his father has the same ambiguity that Eric feels for the Whipper. He has begun to understand his father and to accept his love even while he blames him. He has begun to doubt the existence of a Whipper, yet feels a need to place blame outside himself.

In *Conversations*, Manfred agrees that the Whipper may be a kind of Freudian expression of Eric's subconscious, but says, "I was thinking mostly of setting up a background for Eric Frey and his father. . . . In the sanitorium, he's rather tender and kind to Eric, which I think as time goes on, every son begins to see about his father" (C90). In contrast to the tenderness, Eric recalls the whipping he got from his father for peeking at his mother in the shower—an incident from Manfred's life when he saw his Aunt Kathryn in a shower (C91). Remembering his pain, Manfred created the Whipper in the image of his father. He explains it to John Milton in *Conversations:*

I was overwhelmed by the notion of the great vast spaces and distances around us. Just as the human being can be an orphan, the earth itself is an orphan. At first my thought was that perhaps the universe was chuckling ironically at our little ambitions, our little hopes, our aspirations. But the more I began to see about it, the more I began to see it was more than that; it was probably just indifferent to us all. Whatever we had we made ourselves, and we make the Whipper in our own image. (C 92)

Most reviewers, even those with negative views, praised Manfred for his sincerity, for the authenticity of the book, and for its power. The *New Yorker* reviewer found the style strained and clumsy, the dialogue inept, but found the book to have "considerable if uncontrolled force." (12/1/45) Wendell Johnson, in the *Chicago Sun Book Week* (12/9/45), thought that Manfred sometimes splatters an adjective, overstates a feeling or mood, gives the reader an extra shove he doesn't really need in order to appreciate the intended effect; but he sees Manfred's integrity and forthrightness as most important, praising his feeling for essential details and respect for characters. The London *Spectator* (9/1/50) reviewer wrote, "Sometimes naive, sometimes vulgar, but the book attains its effect by the complete sincerity that shines from the writer through his hero and all the characters he has created."

Van Wyck Brooks wrote Manfred to say that he found *Boy Almighty* a great advance on *The Golden Bowl* in its unity and continuity of mood. He saw such an effect achieved by Manfred's use of the progress of the disease, his own disease, as the form and the truth of the book.[5] In *The New York Times Book Review* (1/13/46), Nona Balakian wrote, "The author achieves a kind of kaleidoscope of human desires and frustrations that reads like poetry in separate passages."

II Wanderlust *(1962)*

Wanderlust is a revised and shortened version of the trilogy *World's Wanderer*, which includes *The Primitive* (1949), *The Brother* (1950), and *The Giant* (1951). Originally, Manfred had wanted to bring the three books out together, to be read as a unit, but the publisher pushed for separate titles each year. The individual volumes received harsh treatment from "Eastern" critics, and Manfred shifted his attention then from autobiography to the Buckskin Man Tales. It wasn't until 1962 that he had a chance to revise the trilogy and to bring the books together in one volume, called *Wanderlust*, as was his original intention.

Because in *The Primitive* Manfred consistently criticized the Reformed Church and all it stood for, the publication of the book in 1949 caused a stir on the Calvin College campus in Grand Rapids, Michigan, the Christian College of the book. A better understanding of that "stir" and of Manfred's relationship to Calvin is now available in a paper, "Manfred and Calvin College," by Peter Oppewall, professor of English at Calvin College. Oppewall makes a detailed comparison between events and characters in *The Primitive* and those in real life. He admits that even today there is a certain sadness on the campus that Manfred has not moved closer to evangelical Christianity and that he gave up the Frisian name Feike Feikema. Nevertheless, he writes, "There is indeed on Calvin's campus today a large reservoir of good will toward Frederick Manfred," built up largely by his personal appearances on campus. "All who have met him are charmed by his justly famed warmth of personality and sense of humor."[6]

A.   *Book* I: The Primitive

Thurs Wraldson, a Siouxland orphan, is sent to Christian College in Zion, Michigan, by Mrs. Brothers, the orphanage director, who expects him to become a preacher. The trip out with neighborhood boys is a revelation to Thurs, who has never traveled. His classes, too, are a revelation, for he learns much about himself and human nature. He flunks freshman English, but has a story printed in the school paper; he rejects the fundamentalist doctrines of the church, but comes alive intellectually in the Plato Club, sponsored by his philosophy professor; he is the butt of jokes because of his great height, but becomes a hero on the basketball court. Toward the end of his college days, his two great loves are also great frustrations to him. He falls in love with Hero Bernlef, whose small size is grotesque beside his great bulk; and he falls in love with music, through Professor Maynard, but finds that music unleashes in him dangerous primitive passions. Seeing a connection between his

creative energy in musical composition and his love for Hero, Thurs
gives up both when he almost kills her in a smothering hug when
she doesn't respond to his music. Upon graduation, Thurs is disenchanted with himself for lack of discipline over his energy and
with the college, which has dismissed Professor Maynard for not
following doctrine. Thurs hitchhikes East.

B.   *Book* II: The Brother

Hitchhiking East, Thurs is picked up by a pimp, who returns him
to Chicago, where he stays with and helps two old ladies. On the
road again, Thurs gets a long ride with a trucker and eventually
lands in Greenwich Village, only to be robbed, propositioned by a
man, and beaten by police. Later, he is rescued from the hobo
jungle by Mrs. Babbas, who stakes him to room and board until he
gets a job with the Hammer Rubber Works. At the factory, he is initiated into the worker's world. He fights boredom, suffers from
dust inhalation, watches a man lose his arm in a machine, and meets
labor organizers, Communists, and underworld characters. Through
Rhoda Hammer, he is initiated into the world of management. She
introduces him to sophisticated society stereotypes, including the
sculptress Sabine, who seduces him. When tests show that Thurs
has artistic talent, he leaves the factory for a warehouse job in
Manhattan, where he lives with Peter Roche, who is a Communist.
Thurs is exposed to Communist propaganda, but resents the way art
is controlled by the party line. Although he likes Bernice Malcolm,
daughter of a factory friend who is a Communist leader, he rejects
both her love and her father's enticements to become a Communist.
Again disenchanted, Thurs hitchhikes West.

C.   *Book* III: The Giant

Heading West from New Jersey, Thurs escapes death in a truck
accident, then gets a ride with a man who takes him to Chicago. He
is picked up out of Chicago by Bruce Farewell, a scientist, who persuades him to work in the Twin Cities as a poll taker. Bruce is
married to Hancy Oxenham, a blueblood from a railroad family.
Thurs moves in with another poll taker, Ring Star, who is a ladies'
man and is disorganized in his personal habits. At the university
library, Thurs meets Eva Nordling, who plays the piano and knows
books and the local intelligentsia. Ring enlists in World War II, and

when Thurs discovers that he is 4F, he marries Eva. Bruce leaves the polling business to Thurs and begins working on the atomic bomb. Eva introduces Thurs to Twin Cities society, and one night at a party, he surprises his friends and himself by playing a part of his original composition, forgotten since college days. Thurs discovers that he is the true son of his former music teacher, Mr. Maynard, and goes to be with him on his deathbed. Knowledge of his parentage seems to release in Thurs his pent-up creative energy. He devotes full time to musical composition and becomes successful. The Wraldsons move to an acreage overlooking the Minnesota River valley. In spite of a brief intrigue Thurs has with a young neighbor girl, he and Eva are brought close together by Eva's pregnancy. When she has to be rushed to the hospital in a storm, Bruce drives and has an accident in which Thurs is fatally injured. The others survive, and Bruce, who was testing a scientific theory while speeding on a curve, blames himself and scientific pride. He hopes that in the next life the ghost of Christ, the haunt of Marx, and the spirit of Scire will deal kindly with us.

Manfred has said that *The Primitive* is 51 percent auto-biographical and 49 percent invented or taken from other people's lives; *The Brother* is perhaps 40 percent autobiographical, and *The Giant* is almost completely changed or invented.[7] For example, he points out that Eva is not his own wife, but is a composite of his wife, his mother, and three other women[8]. Yet events are based on reality: "Naturally, as I went about describing Thurs's and Eva's married life, I laid my hands on any information I could get in the way of concrete details, from my own marriage as well as from (and mostly from) the married lives of friends. . . . Real life is always the final source. Even the genie who composes my night dreams, let alone my daydreams, has to draw from that source"[9].

Eva may not be Manfred's wife, but Thurs is certainly created in Manfred's six foot nine image, and the events of *Wanderlust* follow closely certain events in Manfred's life. The "arch of the work," as Manfred puts it, is made of autobiographical elements: "This means that Thurs as a person in World's Wanderer Wanderlust was created in my own image, after my own likeness. This means that the life or span of life of Thurs was created after my own span or way of life. In the beginning there was my life; and then there was 'Thurs's life,' or the 'new life' (Aristotle's 'imitation'), or the 'second life' "[10].

In being a novel of formation and of the development of the writer as artist, *Wanderlust* could be a work of the type called *bildungsroman* or, more precisely, *kunstlerroman*, in the pattern of Joyce's *Portrait of the Artist as a Young Man* or Proust's *Remembrance of Things Past*. But there is a problem in this classification, since Thurs is a musician and not a writer. In *Conversations*, Manfred explains that, but for a twist of fate, he might have been a composer rather than a writer. He had perfect pitch and reacted strongly to music. He describes listening to the Minneapolis Symphony playing Tchaikovsky: "Something in me suddenly awoke and wanted to get out of me. And I literally had tremors of fire running up and down my backbone. I thought I was going to go wild. I had an impulse to jump up and start skipping over the tops of seats. I wanted to jump up into the gallery. I really thought I was going out of my mind there for a little" (C164). Thurs has a similar reaction when he attends a concert with Hero and fears that someone may have noticed his behavior.

Manfred sees a strong connection between music and literature, and in having Thurs develop as a composer, he sees a parallel to his own development as a writer. He says in *Conversations* that the structure of *Wanderlust* is based on Beethoven's First Symphony, with its three movements and recurring themes. Throughout the trilogy, one can find repetitions of characters, themes, and symbols, often accented by a naming pattern. "The very sounds of the words themselves, I saw, could be employed as if they were notes of music," he writes in the postscript to *The Giant*[11]. There are repeated "helper" figures, such as Ring Star and Howard Starring and William Rexford; there are untouchable "white goddess" figures, such as Hero and Helen; there are mother figures, such as Mrs. Brothers and Mrs. Babbas; and there are wife figures, such as Eveling and Eva. Thurs himself is identified with the oversized pileated woodpecker he finds with wings broken in New York. Out of place and hurt among the bank buildings of lower Manhattan, the woodpecker is like Thurs, whose directions get switched at the sight of parks or the sound of train whistles. But back in Minnesota and in command of his art, Thurs sees a happy pair of these birds, and Ring, visiting during leave from the army, greets him with, "And you, you old pileated woodpecker you . . ." (672).

However, more basic to the musical motif than such repetitions is the playing of the initiation theme in three movements, with Thurs exposed first to Christianity, then to communism, and finally to science. Through his ordeal with each, Thurs holds in check his creative passion, until in the final section, titled "Explosion," he rejects all three for his art. Manfred has Thurs say: "I mean it is the composer, the creator, who is the real king. I'm a democrat and all that, but I'm willing to argue that an original, a creator, comes pretty close to being the only real aristocrat we have. And I'm also enough of a democrat to believe that the originals can be born anywhere, in any family, high on the economic scale or low. Orphanages. Anywhere" (611).

Christianity and communism fail in similar ways, as Thurs elaborates at the close of *The Brother*, in a paragraph which ends, "Ergo: Marxism is as much a religion as Christianity and as such can also be considered an opium of the people" (510). Science, in the person of Bruce, fails Thurs and destroys him, as science can also destroy mankind. Only art provides salvation for Thurs and, Manfred would suggest, for us all.

As his father is dying, Thurs reflects on his own life, the ties and connections in it: "Life *was* a symphony with its chords and themes constantly appearing and reappearing" (647). In Manfred's own life, there was a happy replaying of themes when he returned to Calvin College in 1959 for a class reunion. Calvin hadn't been very friendly to him, especially after *The Primitive* came out, so he was unprepared for the enthusiastic reception he got from students. In a spur of the moment answer to a student's question, he came to an understanding about the relationship between theology and art. Thus, in a return to the setting of the novel, he picked up on a theme in the book and played a variation on it, telling students that among the many paths to God, art was as good as theology: "In the final analysis I thought that perhaps God was a very great artist, a greater artist than he was a theologian" (C169).

Manfred was pleased to find that he could come home again to his alma mater. Thurs the young composer and Manfred the young writer may have offended by seeming always to put themselves in the right and the professors in the wrong. An older Manfred says of Thurs, "In some ways he was wrong too" (C168). The history of the trilogy would suggest that Manfred, too, saw himself as guilty of some of the same errors of exuberance that plagued Thurs.

World's Wanderer, as the early trilogy was titled, received harsh treatment from the "Eastern" critics, who saw Manfred as unable to separate himself from the grotesqueries of his protagonist. They did not like his playing with the language, his cute references to contemporaries in name coinages, his tendency to mix the burlesque with the serious. Manfred agrees with the evaluation of Alan Swallow, publisher of *Wanderlust*, who saw *World's Wanderer* as essentially a rough draft. "I had the problem of knowing too much before I began," Manfred says (C162). Where the author of *World's Wanderer* was like the Thurs of Christian College, the author of *Wanderlust* is more like the Thurs whose symphonies are played by the Minneapolis orchestra. Because he has more experience, he can be more selective, can depend less upon tricks with language and more upon consistent style, and can avoid blatant stereotyping in favor of authentic characterization.

In *Conversations*, John Milton wonders if Manfred has achieved in *Wanderlust* some kind of union between craftsmanship and vision. Certainly the new trilogy gives us a unique example of how an author can reduce and shape his raw material, but it also establishes the Manfred vision as it is expressed in various themes. An exploration of the vision and the themes will make up the final portion of this book, where there will be a consideration of primitivism, of the quest for the father, of the importance of place and the meaning of rootedness, of the male-female relationship, of the role of the artist in society, and of the search for self.

In commenting upon his purpose in writing *Wanderlust*, Manfred says it is the story of a man's search for ultimate happiness, of his not finding it in religion, or in social systems, or in science, and then going "back to childlike worship, the search for beauty . . . no, not the search for beauty, but the expression of beauty that he finds within himself. I think that the remarkable thing about it is that he finds it within himself" (C166 - 67).

III   Green Earth *(1977)*

Green Earth was published after the manuscript of this book had been completed. Therefore, the attention given this "rume" is not as detailed as the book deserves. Manfred says he had been keeping notes for such a book about his parents even while he was a student at Calvin College. As the years went by, the file on the book grew to great length, and Manfred worked on it at a leisurely pace, thinking that it might be a book left for publication after his own death. Perhaps he decided to bring it out earlier than that because both his father and his Aunt Kathryn had died the previous year, his father at the age of ninety after an idyllic third marriage.

Green Earth and *Wanderlust* together are a fictional rendition of the author's life from birth through early manhood. *Boy Almighty* is also a rume, sharply focused on the two years Manfred spent in a tuberculosis sanitorium in the early 1940s. *Green Earth*, however, is much more thoroughly autobiographical than the other rumes. Manfred says that Alfred (Free) Alfredson, the central figure, is more nearly a portrait of himself than are any of his other characters.

Green Earth is the story of the green years of Free as he grows to maturity on a farm in Siouxland (northwest Iowa) during the twenty years between 1909 and 1929. But it is also the story of Free's mother and father and of their relatives—the Englekings and the Alfredsons. Ada Engleking, the mother, is a woman of strict Christian upbringing and of delicate sensibilities, while Alfred Alfredson, the father, is a strong but good illiterate whose own father was a freethinker. As Ada and Alfred fall in love, marry, and farm as renters on several places, they forge a bond of mutual respect that enables them to face the hardships of poverty and weather as well as the pettiness of the people around them. Where Alfred gives up his own church affiliation and his fiddle playing, Ada learns to accept her husband's illiteracy and his manly ways. Free is the first of five boys born to the couple, and it is largely through his sensibilities that the events in their lives are recorded.

In those individual events themselves, as in the lives they define, sorrow and joy, good and bad balance out. For example, Free experiences the joy of learning in a one room country school along with the pain of punishment from his father when he skips school; he has the pride of reading aloud daily from the Bible along with the sorrow of humbling his father, who cannot read; he has the exhilaration in hard work well done, as well as the resentment in seeing hard work go unrewarded; he has the excitement of sexual discovery along with the guilt and fear associated with early sexual explorations; he has the thrill of imagination triggered by reading along with the ridicule such intellectual adventures provoked in relatives and friends; he has the exuberance of play with brothers and friends balanced by the satisfaction in cherished moments of solitude.

The point of view shifts at times from Free to Ada or Alfred, but Free is the "ground" of the novel for which Ada and Alfred share the "cultivating." Much of the tension is created as the influence of one or the other parent seems to be shaping Free's personality. In the end, again, a balance seems to be struck. In *Conversations with Frederick Manfred*, the novelist says of his mother, "She had a tremendous influence on me. Not as much as my father. My father had the most influence in the long run" (C24). Nevertheless, *Green Earth* is dedicated to Manfred's mother.

Those who have read most of Manfred's books will be intrigued with the glimpses given in *Green Earth* of characters who have been given portraiture in other novels. For example, we get just a brief acquaintance with the hired man Garrett Engleking, whose story is told more fully in *The Man Who Looked Like the Prince of Wales*. Free's Aunt Karen and her husband Kon are principal characters in *Eden Prairie*. The setting and the lifestyles in *The Chokecherry Tree* are similar to those in *Green Earth*.

Now that *Green Earth* has been published, earlier novels that seemed autobiographical are shown to be less so than they seemed. Alfred and Ada are not Pier and Nertha of *This is the Year*, though the setting of the novel and many of its incidents and characters come from the author's experiences as a boy. Likewise, *The Chokecherry Tree* is not truly autobiographical.

Green Earth is Manfred's best rume. In it he has done most of the things he said in the postscript to *Giant* that a rumester must do. He has taken the inner logic of his life as a model or central idea around which he has constructed an intense and highly personal story out of heartfelt agonies and successes. He successfully imagines himself as the very young Free adjusting to the physical world, and he then performs the difficult task of shifting the point of view gradually through the novel as Free becomes more sophisticated and aware of his intellect.

In the seven hundred twenty-one pages of *Green Earth*, Manfred has shown us what it was like to grow up in mid-America during the first quarter of this century. Some readers will find certain details of that growing up ugly or crude, as the author anticipates in his Preface, but again, a balance is struck. In striving to render the totality of a life lived, Manfred is giving his regional novel characteristics of universality. In discussing the "rume," he says that he feels as he works that he is doing something "holy and passionate," that he feels somewhat as the ancient runesters must have felt when they slashed their single strokes on a tree or stone: "Here, this now, this we must record. Today. It is not all of our lives. But it catches up as much as a single stroke can what is most us in this singular moment" (*Giant* 409).

Green Earth is such a stroke. It is the author's "mark"—single, as Free is a single individual, but a mark that nevertheless contains a wealth of information. The details of that information attracted the attention of reviewers.

For *Publisher's Weekly* (9/19/77), the reviewer wrote, "Manfred does stretch some of his scenes excessively, but his insistent accumulation of detail somehow gives the novel a compelling kind of life." The writer for *Kirkus Reviews* (9/1/77) said that Manfred had the compulsion, once the plow tip digs into sites and characters, to "detail every event, talk, or beard scratch as far as the eye can see," but he goes on to say that reading *Green Earth* is like "watching grass grow, even and unaccented, yet somehow impressive as the prairie, all salt and sweat and earth rooted."

In his review for the *Minneapolis Tribune* (11/27/77), Russell Roth wrote:

Green Earth is the epitome of Manfred: a strong and compelling story that gains rather than loses power and momentum from its ever-accumulating mass of interwoven detail. It is meticulously historical, larger-than-life in its characterizations, and full of a Rabelais-cum-Breughel good humor in its depiction of a humanity still rooted in and drawing its primary force—whether willingly or not—from the soil.

Roth singles out the mother, Ada, as one of the most memorable of Manfred's characters, a saintly woman who paradoxically, in drawing her strength into the men of her family, becomes more "earth mother" than saint. In a poem titled "Mother," written in 1934, Manfred writes of his mother, Alice, to whom *Green Earth* is dedicated: "Your gift was the cradle in the fleshen mold, / Your gift was blood and race and ancient right."[12]

In memory of his father, dead at ninety years, Manfred wrote a poem titled "Where Is Everybody," in which the old man reflects back over the years Manfred has described in *Green Earth*. Here is the second stanza:

> Where is everybody?
> Nobody around I know.
> Nobody I can talk old times with—
> squareskips I used to call in country barns,
> that baseball game at Alvord
> where they tagged a guy out at home
> with a potato,

the time I accidentally jabbed
a hayfork into my knee,
the time I fell seventy feet
off the cupola on Reynold's round barn
and lived because I landed
in a pile of cowshit six feet deep,
the first time I slept with a woman
which was your mother Alice,
the time I had to beg crumbs in Lebanon, Missouri,
because your grampa was out of work.
Where is everybody?[13]

IV   Morning Red (1956)

Until *Milk of Wolves* was published in 1976, *Morning Red* seemed to be, among Manfred's novels, a solitary example of the long novel in counterpoint, what he calls a "romance." As with the more recent *Milk of Wolves*, publishers were shy of the long manuscripts, and small presses were found to bring them forth. *Morning Red* was begun in April of 1951, but work on it was interrupted in December of 1952, so that Manfred could finish *Lord Grizzly*, the book that would give a new direction to his career. Thus *Morning Red*, though published in 1956, is akin to the earlier Manfred of the trilogy and shares some of the faults of those books. An end note reports continuation of work on the book between March 1954 and June 1955, with completion in February 1956. *Morning Red*, though somewhat tedious and bizarre, is a valuable book for Manfred scholars because it is a catalogue of the author's ideas.

Morning Red is two stories in counterpoint—the stories of Kurt Faber and Jack Nagel, who were Northland College roommates. Kurt Faber is a country boy from South Dakota who takes a job on the *Brokenhoe News* in a suburb of the Twin Cities in Minnesota. Jack Nagel, son of Earl Nagel, the beer baron, suffers from a head wound received in World War II and wants to write plays. The two are opposites. Where Kurt is blond, Jack is dark; where Kurt is robust and positive about life, Jack is weak and negative, the victim of an overprotective mother and a bull of a father.

A tornado strikes near a hospital where Jack is a patient. In the confusion, he rapes a helpless woman, Elizabeth Watkins, and carries her out into the storm, to his home and then to Minnehaha Falls, where he rapes her again.

Kurt, meanwhile, has gotten involved in local politics and has met Grace Borgen, daughter of the owner of Borgen Bakeries, Brokenhoe's major industry. When his friend Win Owens is beaten up by the Duum boys, Kurt gets Monk Edwards, a Siouxland friend, to be Win's lawyer. Monk is also the public defender for Jack Nagel, who has been jailed for rape. Kurt, who observes the connection between the political bosses and the underworld, refuses to run for mayor when asked to run by friends.

In preparing to defend Jack, Monk visits Liz Watkins, who lives in Bonnie, Monk's Siouxland hometown. Liz, whose marriage opportunities have been foiled because of sexual inhibitions, lives with her mother and runs the Bonnie Post Office. She has a suspiciously close relationship to her brother Walt, who gets her confused with his wife Lilibet. Monk's visit brings back to him memories of his own tragic life as a doctor in the community. He had been victimized by Mrs. Pierce, the local do-gooder, who had had him castrated by a mob. Monk causes Liz to reconsider her position with respect to Jack.

Meanwhile, Kurt has decided to run for mayor so that he can marry and support Grace Borgen. He gets caught in a dirty political campaign, is forced to do things he instinctively hates, and loses—but his votes help elect a party man to the state senate. Kurt's paper prospers, and he moves easily into high society. However, at a party Jack's sister Fon gives for her brother, Kurt fights Fon's husband for making passes at Jack's wife, Jill.

Jack has had enough and decides to drop out of his family forever, changes his name to Jon Aldringham, and gets help from his father's black valet, who seems more creative and free than the wealthy Jack. Back in Bonnie, Liz finally accepts her old boy friend, Bert, and drops charges against Jack.

Kurt's romance falls apart when he learns that Grace is a whore and that her father got his start with gangster money. As he leaves her house, four mobsters beat him up and dump him in a swamp.

In a fit of depression, Jack had tried to kill himself by jumping into the Mississippi River. But he was rescued by Anna Marie, who lived alone as a squatter on Northland Coal property along the river. When the Northland people destroy her home, Jack again tries to jump from Washington Bridge, but he is saved this time by Kurt. However, Jack steals Kurt's gun and confronts his father, having realized finally that Dad Nagel is the controlling power behind the mob, the politicians, and Northland Coal. Jack shoots his father and himself.

Kurt is given Jack's car and cat, and on the way home in a snow storm resolves to have the guts to be a good journalist, a watchman.

Two keys to full appreciation of *Morning Red* are in the fact that Manfred subtitles it "a romance" and in the device of "doubling" he uses. These stylistic and structural configurations allow him to present a full range of contrasting characters in developing bold psychological and political concepts.

The romance label sets up a number of connotations. It suggests Hawthorne and his definition of a romance in the preface to *The House of Seven Gables*; it recalls the "love story" formula in popular women's magazines or in gothic romances; and it also puts Manfred in the tradition of such mainstream American writers as Hawthorne, Poe, Melville, Twain, and Faulkner. *Morning Red*, in fact, is dedicated to William Faulkner, and at one point in the story, some characters are said to be from Yoknapatawpha County.

Because Manfred deliberately calls *Morning Red* a romance, he would seem to be claiming the same latitude as to fashion and material that Hawthorne claims. He wants to be free to make his plot turn on coincidence, as in the meeting of Kurt and Jack on the bridge to avoid Jack's suicide; he wants to feel free to use melodrama and the grotesque, as with Monk's punishment and unusual surgery or with Anna Marie's tonguelessness; he wants freedom to let characters expand into psychological archetypes, as Monk becomes a Christ figure, Earl Nagel the ruthless human bull, Jack the obsessed poet playing with force, Jill the modern female, and so forth. In the final pages, Manfred, perhaps unnecessarily, has Monk run down the cast of characters, identifying the archetypal role of each[14].

A look at Manfred's papers on *Morning Red* in the University of Minnesota Archives indicates that he was making an effort to tie his characters to a "familiar world," even though many critics, including his friend John K. Sherman, complained about his "incredible" characters. In a response to Sherman, published in the *Minneapolis Tribune* (12/16/56), Manfred replied that he had "many clippings, notes, and documents to support everything in the novel, including the language and the dialogue."

For example, the grotesque surgery Monk performs on himself is documented by a *Time* article (4/2/45) in which a similar operation was performed by a Dr. Frumkin of Russia. The file includes stories and articles about a woman raped in a hospital bed; about a boy who killed his mother because she repressed his sex life; about the exploits of Isadore Blumenfeld (Kidd Cann), an underworld character prominent in the Twin Cities; about political corruption and underworld activities in several large cities; about psychological research dealing with sexual habits and mores.

By calling his book a romance, then, Manfred set up a context which will have an affinity with tragedy, with the tragic emotions of passion and fury, with the supernatural and the mystical; and at the same time, he tries to surround his reader with familiar events and characters derived from daily newspaper accounts.

While using the conventions of the romance, Manfred at the same time tells a double story. At one point in the Anna Marie episode, he has Jack take note of an open book lying on a sewing machine. It is *Anna Karenina.* Jack tells Anna Marie: "It's like a molar. Two roots in a single crown. . . . It's really neither Anna's story nor Levin's. The counterpoint is all" (580).

The two roots in *Morning Red* are Kurt's story and Jack's story, crowned as they are by the figure of Monk, in whose person the two themes are blended and the counterpoint established. Actually, as Manfred relates in *Conversations, Morning Red* began as two books, one called *The Rape of Elizabeth* and the other *Mountain of Myrrh.* When both his wife and his friend Russell Roth told him that the two stories had the same tone, Manfred decided that he could get the most out of them in combination: "So I then threw everything away, made a brand new plot, sketched it all out, what I wanted to do . . ." (C74).

It seems he wanted to strike a balance between two types of male personality, the one type highly intelligent but flawed and vulnerable because of excessive mother love, and the other less intelligent but able to survive through a gutsy use of his natural instincts.

Through Jack Nagel, Manfred shows us what happens to a personality unable to bring his psyche into balance. Jack cannot face his external world, cannot cope with his guilt feelings, and is at the mercy of his passions. Kurt, on the other hand, represents an ego that has achieved some harmony. Without both stories, the book would present an unbalanced view, tilted too much either toward the neurotic or toward the normal.

Also, by putting the two stories together, Manfred is able to set up another contrast to be harmonized by Monk—that between city and country. Jack is city bred and suffers from urban conditions; Kurt is country bred and is thus more open and flexible; Monk is a man of both worlds and able to reconcile the two.

The technique of doubling permeates the entire novel, not only in the characters of Kurt and Jack, but in several other pairings as well. For example, the two sisters, Elizabeth and Lilibet, are linked together through Walt, who appears to have made love to both and who calls both "Liscious." Liz is bright faced, has bluebell eyes, is snippish with men; Lilibet is sad faced, has languid hazel eyes, is easy with men. Furthermore, the essential Siouxland wholesomeness of Liz can be contrasted with the blemished Grace—whose physical ailment may be a feminine counterpart to the mental anguish of Jack, both victims of corrupt environments. Walt and Jack may be seen as a pair having Elizabeth and thumb sucking in common. Liz thinks of Walt when Jack makes love to her at the falls. Polly's city-bred cheating may be contrasted with Butts' Indian-bred simple honesty, especially as seen in the two family dinners Kurt attends; and Kurt sees Polly as a surrogate for his brother Bill, who is a tempter to evil. Jack sees Sumner Ford, his father's black valet, as a better father figure than Dad Nagel because Ford is a creator rather than a collector. Toward the end of the book, Jack begins to take on a physical resemblance to Monk, with his white hair and beard, suggestive of their common lack of masculinity. Finally, Aunty Vee, Jack's liberated relative, can be seen as a balance against the intolerance of Mrs. Pierce.

Central in both stories is the theme of love, ironically in its romantic sense as "love story" but realistically in its psychological sense as sexual adjustment. The characters whose lives are maladjusted are pictured as incomplete or out of proportion. Jack tells Ford late in the book that he never had it in him to make it: "I wasn't man enough. There was too much woman in me. And boy not become man. Imagine! my whole life soured, spoiled, because I wasn't born with the right proportion. 40 - 60 instead of 60 - 40. Oh I tried all right. I tried. But I just couldn't finish a single solitary thing"(521). Jack feels bottled up and prays just before the rape scene, "Please, God, please help me open the flood gates"(73). Then, as he leaves Elizabeth's room after the rape, he thinks to himself, "Whole again" (77).

Elizabeth, too, is incomplete and, without being aware of it, is made "whole again" through her experience with Jack, especially when they make love under the falls—symbol of free-flowing passion, of opening the flood gates of repression.

This coming together of incompletes is representative of the explanation of love Plato reports in the *Symposium*, quoted in some detail by Monk and Kurt as they philosophize over Jack's condition. That love is the "good" is made clear as Monk continues quoting from the *Symposium*: "Wherefore let us exhort all men to piety, that we may avoid the evil and obtain the good, of which Love is the lord and leader" (565).

In being good, love should also be pleasurable, Manfred suggests, and should not be thwarted. To thwart love is to do evil, to become love's opposite, as Mrs. Pierce becomes. Monk sees her as a professional virgin: "Somewhere back, had she married the right man, and had she raised a brood of children, and had she enjoyed love, she might have become one of those strong dominant mothers one oftentimes sees in the country" (168).

Monk can see makings of a Mrs. Pierce in Elizabeth, who is afraid to enjoy sex. "But in God's eyes enjoyment of flesh is a sin," she tells him. Monk tells her God intended sex to be pleasurable to guarantee the propagation of mankind, that sex without having children is not a waste since billions of seeds are wasted by God's design, that the stream must be kept flowing, that the sex drive is as sublime as mother love (363).

Manfred wants to raise fatherhood to the same high level that motherhood enjoys. He has Monk describe women as "holders" and men as "probers." Thus he sees women as more than mere vessels, for holding is an active, not a passive art. And he sees men as more creative than women, being more free, for it is the prober in man that makes him erect towers, build buildings, write symphonies, or explore nature (563). Man is also more vulnerable to warping than woman and can fall, as Jack did.

Jack's failure, Manfred suggests, is in part the result of his overreliance on intellect as opposed to the instinctual. Monk tells Justin Teague, the district attorney: "All of us who've made law and justice our career . . . should never forget how deeply the primal drives of life are rooted in each of us, should remember our common animal origin every time we get a so-called sick person on our hands. Before we condemn we ought to remember what we ourselves are" (544 - 45). Monk sees Jack's unhappiness as a symbol of our times, where emotions are dammed up and sacrificed to intellect. In speaking to John Milton about Jack in *Conversations*, Manfred says:

You take the Christian who says man is by nature prone to sin and to do evil, or the evolutionist who says man is by nature prone to be an

animal—they're both right. That is man's real nature. All the other business
is whitewash. Intellectuality. There is just a little piece of the intellectual in
man. A little piece of whitewash. And as he does climb toward that intellectuality—and it does seem that he wants to go toward that little streak of
light up there—he runs into all sorts of horrible problems. He has to get rid
of the natural instincts he has and replace them with something else. He
begins by being one thing and then winds up being something else. And
the turning and pulling is just a little too much. The crest is too high. So he
snaps. And I mean to show that snapping. Man will survive all right. (C77 -
78)

Man's survival, Monk says, will be through that primal opposite
to hate, love. Even though Justin calls love a goosey word, Monk
still has faith in it and argues for better education about sex and
motherhood (546).

In Jack's story an individual is brought to destruction through
personal failure to overcome the accident of birth; in Kurt's story an
individual is threatened with destruction from a diseased society,
but through personal strength, survives. Early in Kurt's story, the
local mobster, Dink, explains to Kurt that he might as well take a
bribe because "even big business is a racket these days"(69). Kurt
still says "No."

Kurt maintains his idealism stubbornly, but when there seems to
be a chance to marry Grace if only he had money, Kurt agrees to
run for mayor on underworld money. In a dream, The Very
Reverend Thorstein Ingersoll lectures him on the sad state of
politics in which both parties tell nothing but lies (457). But Kurt
doesn't understand the full scope of corruption until Jack in the
final scene with him reveals that his father, Earl Nagel, is not only
in control of both the cereal and liquor industries but bosses the law
officials as well as the underworld. Completely cynical now, Jack
says: "Maybe that's the way society gets its business done. Maybe
love and rules are wrong. Maybe it's best that one has friends with
influences, contacts, inside dope, to get things done, and not laws"
(570 - 71).

Jack fails to some extent because he cannot cope with the real
world, cannot tolerate imperfection any more than he can his wife's
snoring. Kurt survives because he learns through experience to see
how good and evil are not so easily separated; he sees how good can
come from evil, as in the rejuvenation of the *Brokenhoe News*, or
how evil can come from an effort to do good, as in the example of
Mrs. Pierce. Although Manfred, through Kurt, sympathizes with

the more liberal Democratic or, in Dad Hildebrand's political lexicon, "darkbread" point of view, it is in the Democratic party that the corruption is pictured. The good isn't all on one side. Kurt in fact likes the man he opposes for mayor.

It is just here, in this recognition of the coexistence of opposites, that the counterpoint of meaning is established through both stories. For example, it is possible for Elizabeth to be pious and still enjoy sex. The duality is all. Even among the sexes, a healthy mixture is found; as Monk says, "Now, there are very few men who are pure male and there are few women who are pure female"(563). Manfred puts it another way in an interview with Peter De Boer: "I want all my rooms to connect." [15]

Kurt's understanding of both the sexual and the political realities is symbolized in the final episode of the book as he struggles to get home to Brokenhoe through a snow storm, driving Jack's old car and carrying his cat. In order to get through, he has to leave the road and cut across the fields. "In a storm who was to say any man had to stick to the straight and narrow, the highway"(607). He learns that good and evil mix when he is forced to spend the night with a farmer, who turns out to be the "good" brother of Buck and Dern Duggan, who gave Kurt his horrible beating in the city. If the storm itself symbolizes the grief and evil in life that man must face, it also symbolizes the good, the beautiful. "Hearty old earth had become a soft white maiden," Kurt observes (614). It is in being able to see both aspects of the storm, of life, that Kurt is prepared to pass safely through the drift. Manfred sets Kurt's perspective against Jack's response to the storm that opens the book, in which he loses control. In seeing life only one way, Jack is as perverted as Mrs. Pierce. He can see no good in his father, but Kurt can. But perhaps Jack is not to be blamed. He is an accidental victim of the storm, of life, whereas Kurt is a disciplined victor.

Comfortable out of the storm in the Duggan guestroom, Kurt assesses his life and sees himself to be a journalist—a watchman. "Of course, it would take guts to be a watchman. Among other things, it might mean baring the human heart on occasion. And no man looked forward to the job of pointing out the sins and vanities men had in common . . ." (613). Remembering his disciplined father, he is glad to inherit that discipline—and so he dreams.

In his dream he hears a voice out of Isaiah saying, "Set a watchman, ye fabers, and eat, and drink and anoint the shield." The watchman hears the message that Babylon is fallen. Asked,

"What of the night?" the watchman replies, "The morning comes
and also the night." The final line of the dream is, "The burden of
the valley of vision," which is the first line of Isaiah 22. Thus Kurt
as journalist, and one can assume Manfred as novelist, takes on the
burden of the watchman who sees the coming of night and day,
good and evil. It is a tough role to play, but as Kurt says in blasting
through that last snow drift, "Sure we'll make it! . . . C'mon, baby,
gimme some guts"(616).

Negative criticism of *Morning Red* centered on its improb-
abilities, its complexities, and its sermonizing; positive criticism approved its truth and power, its social criticism, and its management
of theme.

Just as critics of Jack's play, "The Snake and the Dove," found it
"completely improbable," so some critics of *Morning Red* found it
"strong but incredible," in John K. Sherman's words. In his thesis
on Manfred, Peter De Boer complains that the "marvellous" effects
are in fact ridiculous. De Boer also criticizes the book's complexity.
He thinks it includes building blocks of so many shapes, sizes, and
varieties that structure is destroyed and the novel becomes a
"dumping ground for a host of Manfredian truths."[16]

In a similar vein, Victor Hass writes in the *New York Times Book
Review* (2/17/57) that stubbornness and lack of discipline have
been pushed to intolerable length. Andrew Schiller, in the *Chicago
Sun Times* (12/30/56), faults Manfred for trying to say everything
and for plotting that is far-fetched and melodramatic. However, he
recognizes memorable scenes and sharp insights.

Novelist Vardis Fisher liked *Morning Red*. In his newspaper
column he wrote: "In this Manfred novel there is more of the stuff
that makes up the lives of most Americans, at least west of the
Mississippi, than a half dozen novels that hit the best seller lists."[17]

Manfred himself has ambivalent feelings about *Morning Red*. He
has written the following inscription on the fly leaf of the archives
copy, dated January 2, 1959:

In the book I dove deeper into the subconscious of man than in any other. I
wasn't too well equipped in this first deep dive, and the book shows it. But
you have to go down sometime, and so I dove. It is in many ways the most
ambitious—and the least successful. I consider it a wonderful "failure" or
an "interesting success," both. The architect who designed the book did all
right—it was the contractor who built it who didn't come up to the job.[18]

V   Milk of Wolves *(1976)*

In *Milk of Wolves,* Manfred has presented a companion piece to *Morning Red:* both books are romances, both deal with life in the Twin Cities in the first half of the century, both also contain rural interludes for contrast, and both deal with the impact of sex on major characters. Much of what was written about the "romance" in the *Morning Red* section also applies to *Milk of Wolves,* especially in the stylization of characters and in the latitude Manfred takes with his material; thus, his new book will likely run into criticisms similar to those leveled at *Morning Red.* It also has some of the same virtues.

Unfortunately, not many people have had an opportunity to read *Milk of Wolves* because of a small first printing of only 2,300 copies. When New York publishers were reluctant to accept such a long novel, a small Boston firm, Avenue Victor Hugo, accepted the challenge and designed a unique format—two columns on eight and one half by eleven stock, running two hundred and fifty pages, divided into two books: *Villain in the City* and *Hermit in the Woods.*

Born in the village of Hackberry Run, Siouxland, Juhl Melander gets a job in a local stone quarry as a blacksmith, but soon he learns the stonecutting trade from Old Cyril and also begins to sculpt heads in granite. When his girl begins to talk of marriage, he leaves for Minneapolis and St. Paul, where he takes a job as stonemason with Bill Jammer. He sculpts and seduces a series of models, including finally a wealthy swimming star, Jessica Savage, whom he marries. They have two children, Philip and Naemi. Eventually, Juhl becomes famous as a sculptor, but his marriage begins to fail because of interference by his mother-in-law, Mrs. Savage.

Juhl moves out of the house and into his studio, where he seduces and sculpts Hallie Phelan, daughter of Judge Phelan. The marriage, though, is patched together for awhile, but is threatened again when money runs out because Juhl works only on a dream project. Jessica has to go to work as a swimming teacher. Juhl tries to enlist in the navy for World War II but is rejected as unstable. He instead becomes a lumberjack in northern Minnesota, where he is befriended by a family of Finns who teach him to appreciate nature. His idyll in the woods ends when he is seriously injured in a sled accident, but the insurance money helps him build a new studio. When

Juhl has an affair with the judge's younger daughter (Poodie), a family fight ensues, because his son Philip loves Poodie and resents his father's behavior. Juhl trades a statue for an island in the Lake of the Woods and abandons his family.

At the opening of Book II, Juhl, with the help of the Assiniboine Indian Wulf Stoneboiler and his family (wife Yvette and twins Faunce and Flur), builds a cabin on his island and a canoe. He follows nature's way, acquires a pet wolf, and enjoys his solitude. When Wulf's wife gets a fever, Wulf walks across the ice for help but joins her in death following the long walk. Even though Juhl gets permission from Faunce to marry Flur, Faunce remains jealous and frustrated. Juhl and Flur lead an idyllic life: Juhl carves figures in the island rocks, and Flur gives birth to their baby in the Indian way. The island paradise cannot last, however, for it is threatened by the jealousy of Faunce and the power of the government, which is forcing Juhl to sell the island to make room for a highway. While Juhl is briefly away, Faunce kills Flur and himself, but the hurt baby lives. Desperate to feed the baby, Juhl cuts his own breast and lets the baby suck blood. Eventually, milk comes. When Juhl has to give up the island, he starts across the lake with the baby and his belongings in a small boat. A storm comes up, the boat capsizes, and the baby drowns. Juhl is rescued and learns that he will get $50,000 for the island—enough to start over again in Siouxland. He is content.

Where in *Morning Red* Manfred achieved a counterpoint effect by dovetailing stories of two contrasting characters, in *Milk of Wolves* he sets up counterpoint by contrasting two environments, the city and the wilderness, as they are experienced by his male artist-hero.

The maleness of the hero is important. Manfred puts a sharp focus on masculinity in *Milk of Wolves*, expanding on his treatment of the role of the father in *King of Spades;* but he is also exploring the creative process and the role of the artist in society. He shows us the archetypal male in several roles—as artist, as father and husband, as lover or lover of sex, and most importantly, as animal—the male animal. As Manfred puts Juhl Melander through his paces, we are shown the interrelationships among these roles and the impact on the hero of environment, both civilized and primitive.

1. *The Male as Animal*

Manfred's emphasis on maleness is a way of returning again to his "old lizard" theme, reminding us of our origins in animal and even plant life—the long view, as John Milton has labeled the theme. When *Milk of Wolves* opens, Juhl contemplates a hike to the source of the Big Rock River; as the book closes, he makes that hike, thinking, "A man should have a picture of his river in his head, all of it"[19]. On this symbolic hike to the source, Juhl stops to look at figures of a man chasing a buffalo that are traced in stone on Buffalo Ridge. He thinks, "Scary thing, seeing those figures there all of a sudden white in the grass, knowing some aborigines made them a long time ago. Makes a man jump a little" (588). The narrative line in *Milk of Wolves* follows Juhl as he walks to his blood source, passing disruptively through the civilized life of the Twin Cities on his way back to primitive ways on Big Wolf Island; but he can't stay on the island either, because he is forced out by both the primitive and the civilized: the Indian Faunce seeks jealous revenge and kills Juhl's ideal partner, Flur; and the highway department confiscates his land in the name of progress. Manfred likely was aware of the warning expressed by D. H. Lawrence in writing about Melville's *Typee* and *Omoo:* "We can't go back. We can't go back to the savages: not a stride. We can be in sympathy with them. We can take a great curve in their direction, onwards. But we cannot turn the current of our life backwards, back towards their soft warm twilight and uncreate mud. Not for a moment. If we do it for a moment, it makes us sick."[20]

As a matter of fact, *Milk of Wolves* may be seen as a working out of the following Laurentian doctrine of blood consciousness: "My great religion is a belief in the blood, the flesh, as being wiser than the intellect. We can go wrong in our minds. But what our blood feels and believes and says, is always true."[21] Harry T. Moore cautions, however, that Lawrence did not advocate "sheer animalism" or the destruction of the mind, that rather he was trying to restore a balance between the intellectual and the emotional side of man.[22]

Nor does Manfred want to eliminate the intellect, but he does use animal ancestors for the contributions they have made to us. Juhl himself is pictured as a "bull" or "bear" of a man, with slender legs and a hairy barrel of a body (56). Early in the story, he is chased by a bull and says to it, "You look like me when I am mad" (8). References to the canine family are frequent, beginning with the family dog and leading to Juhl's close relationship to Three Legged, his pet wolf. Juhl objects to the stylish practice of cutting off a dog's tail and suggests that it is done because humans don't have one:

"Wouldn't it be great if we could all still have our old lost tail?
Human beings will snap at you too if they're hungry enough"(76).
All through the book, Juhl points out the importance of not "getting
your tail down." "The top wolf always has the high tail," he has
observed (57). When Juhl is critically injured and trapped under his
lumber sled, he is tempted to "let his tail down," but a wolf com-
forts him. It puts its nose on Juhl's nose and smells his behind. Encouraged, Juhl chews wood as a beaver would to free himself, thinking, "Funny how a man's mind works. All of a sudden a man can
find himself down in a most awful hole, almost gone, and yet, by
golly, the Old Adam in him will still go to work" (114). Juhl feels it
is a denial of the Old Adam for Jessica to bottle feed their baby:

Well, having the babies out of your bellies it's you who should know that so
long as we remain healthy animals we're still on course. Instead of the route
we're now taking, thinking we're intellectual spirit first and flesh last. As
though our highest goal as man is to become some sort of disembodied nim-
bus. When the body, plainly and simply, is a beautiful thing even when it's
taking a crap. (65)

In contrast to Jessica, Flur wanted to couple as the wolves, not belly
to belly, and to have her baby alone in the snow. Juhl respects the
Indian way and sees Flur's father, Wulf Stoneboiler, to be superior
as a human being because he has the know-how of an animal. Isolated on Big Wolf Island, Juhl reflects on his life:

The stronger the animal in man the better chance he had of getting the best
of his blood into his civilized strategems. That was why he, Juhl Melander,
once of the Cities and before that of Hackberry Run, had chosen to become
a shacker on Big Wolf Island. That he might, somehow, have the animal in
him resurrected. Discover his blood. Instead of having the animal in him
constricted and warped and made mean. Because he had done some mean
low boorish things to his friends. Even villainous. (207)

The above passage suggests the following lines from Whitman:
"The friendly and flowing savage, who is he? / Is he waiting for
civilization, or past it and mastering it?"[23] Whitman, too, longed to
share in the animal virtues. Juhl's retreat to Big Wolf Island may be
seen as a fulfillment of Whitman's wish in the following lines:

I think I could turn, and live with animals, they are so placid and self-
contain'd,
I stand and look at them long and long.

They do not sweat and whine about their condition,
They do not lie awake in the dark and weep for their sins,
They do not make me sick discussing their duty to God,
Not one is dissatisfied, not one is demented with the mania of owning things,
Not one kneels to another, nor to his kind that lived thousands of years ago,
Not one is respectable or unhappy over the whole earth.
So they show their relations to me and I accept them,
They bring me tokens of myself, they evince them plainly in their possession.[24]

In his retreat to Big Wolf Island, Juhl is searching for a kind of original purity to be found in animals. In *The Aristos*, John Fowles has expressed it this way: "Animals lack what we have gained, but we have lost what they still have. We should love them not for their human attributes, but for their innocence. With them we are still in the Garden of Eden; and with ourselves the Fall is every day."[25]

2.   *The Male as Artist*

In turning to live with animals, Juhl rejects Twin City society, where he is a misfit. "I'm the rotten apple, the villain of the piece" (156), he tells Frank III, his lawyer. He sees society as upside down, where money rather than talent establishes the aristocracy. Juhl says that the true aristocrat is the artist, one who cleans up after himself as he goes along: "He tends to be a solitary who tries to do everything alone" (200). As the name "Savage" suggests, Juhl's wealthy mother-in-law is really the savage, the predator, in the worst sense of the term; whereas Wulf Stoneboiler, the Indian, is more to be admired as the true aristocrat. At another sherry opening, Juhl is upset with Leon, an amateur carver, who apologizes for his work. Juhl says to him: "Art comes first. . . . Stand up for your rights. Be a man about it. With these things behind you, you have a right to thumb your nose at kings, man. Even Mrs. Savage. Are you a mouse with a tail between your legs?" (63).

Juhl, of course, follows his own advice; but in standing up for his rights, he tramples on the rights of others and finds he must go it alone. He is both destroyer and creator, just as in carving his statues he must create rubble to reveal the form within. In this respect he is an outsider, an original. Manfred's Juhl Melander is, in fact, a perfect example of Colin Wilson's description of the Outsider:

The Outsider's case against society is very clear. All men and women have these dangerous, unnamable impulses, yet they keep up a pretence, to themselves, to others; their respectability, their philosophy, their religion, are all attempts to gloss over, to make look civilized and rational something that is savage, unorganized, irrational. He is an Outsider because he stands for Truth. . . . The Outsider is a man who cannot live in the comfortable, insulated world of the bourgeois, accepting what he sees and touches as reality.[26]

In explaining his art to the surveyor who comes to estimate the value of his island and its carvings in stone, Juhl says that he cannot put a value on his work: "You see, I don't carve according to the latest fashion. I'm alone. I stand apart. Totally. That's why I want to live on this island. To be in fact and in truth alone. Crap on 'em all" (234). Juhl admits to being arrogant, of never doing anything in reaction to someone else's idea: "He might flare up when people tried to move in on him, but the flaring up was to chase them off, so that he could be all the more true to himself, feel freer to follow his own impulse, to execute sheer Melander inspiration" (57).

It isn't to society that Juhl looks for inspiration but to his instincts and his blood consciousness. Essentially, the source of inspiration is a mystery, a gift that flows up through the body. Juhl tries to explain by saying that he can go just so far intellectually and then must depend upon his fingers for instinctual guidance: "Each finger has an intelligence of its own. A wisdom of the swamp that goes beyond mere brains" (131). Juhl must wait for them to want to take hold again. Yet when he gets the vision from which he creates the nymphs, he finds it was "a scary feeling. Holy. The brain part of him was artist all right, grossly full of bowels as his belly might be. Or perhaps because of the bowels. What a wonder it all was" (80). He faints after completing his sculptures of the nymphs and finds the fainting good, maybe a little like death.

3. *The Male as Lover, Prober*

If creating something true and beautiful can cause a physical response akin to death, so can sexual climax, which has long been seen poetically as "a little death." Juhl senses that this mystery of the creative drive is somehow connected to the sexual drive in the male. In trying to explain how the artist works, he thinks, "It was a lot like knowing whether or not one had made connection with a woman. A man could feel it. It went beyond knowing with the eyes or the root of the tongue" (36).

Even when Juhl regrets some of the mean things he has done, he feels all right about being a "ruttish stud." "The genius in him was located in that," he thinks. "The whole point was to allow the genius stud in him to paw naturally for the white bird fluttering and singing just above him" (207).

Juhl feels that he can get the true form behind the model only after sexual conquest. When Jessica realizes that Juhl has slept with all of his women models, she gets a strange feeling that the bronze face is the true face and that it wasn't just the artist in Juhl but the male in him also that caught the quality of the model. She thinks, "Maybe he had to touch Hallie for one reason or another while sculpting her, like he'd once had to touch her, Jessica, when they first met in his studio" (84). She remembers having read somewhere that a truly great artist tended to be an insatiable lover (56).

Juhl is both pleased with his excessive love making and at the same time bothered by it, for as a result of his ruttish behavior he sees himself as a villain, an outcast. He likes the vision of himself as stallion king and approves of Jessica's assessment of him as a true stallion in not wanting to share his mares with other stallions. When Neda Wildenborg comes along, his "white goddess," he wishes he could sculpt without touching the model. "For once," he says to Neda, "I was hoping I'd really find one of those universals Plato talks about without having it contaminated by the need to touch dross flesh."

"But, goddammit, it's beginning to look like the dirty old Melander in me is right after all . . . that you've got to have a sweet and aching edge-on to sculpt. The two are connected."

"But what about the woman sculptress?" she asked. "If she's good, what does she have?"

"As she sculpts over the stone, her breasts ache and yearn to give suck to the new creature being born under her hands" (128).

Rather than despoil Neda, Juhl finds a man who can bring out in her the necessary spark he wants to capture in stone. He feels that by keeping her pure he can become a god, that the sex route has been too easy (125). Juhl thinks, "Chester might marry and save the fleshly Neda, but Juhl would make and keep forever the true Neda" (131).

4. *The Male as Father*

Juhl was able to keep his hands off Neda, but when Hollie's sister Poodie comes to his studio expecting to be seduced, he reverts back to his rutting ways—and this time it is once too often, because he finds himself in competition with his son Philip. Upon discovering that Juhl has seduced Poodie, Philip attacks his father; then when Jessica tries to stop the stronger Juhl, who could easily hurt Philip, Juhl accuses her, saying, "So now you're on his side, is that it? You're gonna help him kill me, are you?" (142). Later, when Juhl stops Philip from talking to Poodie by ripping out the phone, the two fight again. Mother and daughter pile on to try to separate the men. Calmed down, Juhl realizes that he must leave the family for good. Philip says, "It's about time. Maybe now I'll be able to breathe around here" (154).

This conflict between father and son is a variation on the Oedipus myth Manfred explored in *King of Spades*. He even compares Jessica to Kitty and Philip to Ransom of that book. It is also a replay of the Cronos situation, where the mother Rhea saves the son Zeus from a father fearful that he will be dethroned by his son.

Juhl just doesn't fit into the family as father or as husband, any more than he fits into the larger Twin Cities social whirl. He resents the attention his art attracts to him and claims to be merely a stone cutter, not a sculptor, because, he says, "You come at your work from the bottom up, the humble and doughty, rather than from the top down, high and mighty" (124). Yet Juhl is anything but humble. He is an aristocrat on his own terms, as an artist. He places art above family, in fact sees his "forms" as more true than their models. It seems almost as though Juhl resents women because they create naturally in flesh and blood while he must work in cold stone. When Jessica teases him about making stone ladies, Juhl says,

There you go. So what are you complaining about? You can make live bodies; I can only make lifeless ones. See how much better job you've got compared to what I've got? And then, you don't even give milk to your live creations. When I wish I could to my lifeless ones. (66)

In the end Juhl does give milk to his son in an effort to save him, but the son drowns, and Juhl thinks, "Now I know how a mother feels when she loses a son. No wonder a woman loves a child she's nursed, more than anybody else" (245). These lines echo the final passage in *King of Spades*, "When a son's blood is spilled, which mother weeps the most? The stallions."

In reflecting on why he has chosen to live alone on Big Wolf Island, Juhl tells himself that it is to have the animal in him resurrected, to discover his blood, instead of having the animal in him warped and made mean (207). He learns something about fatherhood from the father wolf that prepares a way for the injured pup; he learns about motherhood from his nursing of baby Wulf; he learns how to be a husband from Wulf Stoneboiler, who sacrifices himself for his wife; he learns, finally, from Flur and the great trees, that he is one with the universe. He finds himself one day under the great trees entranced with the organ sounds, "trying to rhue in tune with the master voice of earth." He sees a family of wolves and says, "They. We. We're all in it together" (186).

Because *Milk of Wolves* has not been represented in the usual review columns, critical appraisal has been lacking. Having had an opportunity to evaluate the book, some reviewers might have found it overly long, two books rather than one, with bizarre events and unrealistic characters. Feminists would object to its celebration of the male at the expense of the female. On the other hand, others might find that the long book nevertheless reads easily, for Manfred is yet the master storyteller, and that the two sections are unified through the personality of Juhl.

VI Arrow of Love *(1961)*

Reading the three novelettes in *Arrow of Love* is a good introduction to the Manfred library. The title story about Indians living in the area of the present Minneapolis and St. Paul, about 1839, is representative of his work in such novels as *Conquering Horse, Scarlet Plume, Lord Grizzly,* and *The Manly-Hearted Woman;* and it fills in another point in the fictional representation of nineteenth century Siouxland, which is the plan of the Buckskin Man Tales. "Lew and Luanne" is so peopled with authentic Siouxland characters as to be classifiable as a rume, or autobiographical story, in the manner of *Wanderlust.* "Country Love," a pastoral, illustrates Manfred's fascination with pairs of characters in contrast, such as he used in *Morning Red.* All of the pieces are, of course, suffused with the sense of the place that is Siouxland.

A. *"Arrow of Love"*

A Sioux brave, Raven, and Opening Rose, a Chippewa, fall in love during a truce at Ft. Snelling. After the truce, Yellowbird and He Washes His Hands kill Goodface, the Sioux chief, in revenge for the earlier killing of their father. In retaliation, Raven and his braves kill all of the encamped Chippewa, including Opening Rose. Then Raven, too, is killed by Yellowbird and He Washes.

Manfred identifies "Arrow of Love" as a romance, and as such it tells a tale of star-crossed lovers from rival families in the tradition of a *Romeo and Juliet*. Superimposed on the romance, however, is the even more powerful Hamlet theme of revenge for the death of a father. As Yellowbird and He Washes prepare to kill Goodface, they seem to have been visited by Striker's ghost. Weeping, Yellowbird says, "Goodface must die. I have dreamed many times and always Striker our father comes, weeping, wanting to know when we will free him so he can depart."[27] After the braves have killed Goodface, Yellowbird dips the image of a woodpecker, Striker's medicine, into Goodface's blood, and He Washes says, "Do not come to us in our dreams now. We wish to be free" (51). The killing seems to be done in response to a deep-seated mystical belief that overrides all personal feeling. The Chippewa braves admired Goodface as a person and say to his little son, Robin, who has watched his father die, "Go, little boy, go home. We do not play war with you. It is only the blood of your father we wanted. We did not wish him dead" (51). This drive for revenge is more powerful even than that of love, as Raven proves, and it is one of the factors which caused the Indians to lose their land.

Raven senses the genocidal aspects of the rivalry between Indian bands when he thinks Opening Rose has been given to Major Kirkland. He thinks: "What fools, what dogs the Sioux and Chippewa were to let themselves be divided by the proud pale ones. The red brothers should smoke the pipe together and agree to destroy the intruder. The drunken yellow hairs were much evil" (29). However, all this wisdom is forgotten when the need for revenge comes upon Raven. He prays to his medicine: "Black one, winged one, raven of my dreams, tell Raven what he should do. Raven is sad. Raven is troubled. Raven wishes to do what is the good thing" (53). Then out of the smoke of his pipe a ghostly vision of Goodface appears, calling for revenge and resolving his indecision.

An opposing voice is heard at the war council from Slow To War, who says:

Raven says we will destroy Leaper's band. Yes. And tomorrow other Chippewa will come down and destroy Goodface's band. And the next day other Dakotah will arise out of the grass and destroy other Chippewa. The killing of the red man by the red man goes on forever. The number of red men grows smaller and smaller. Like the pigeon. While the white man increases. Like the sparrow. (55)

When Leaper speaks at the mass funeral for his dead loved ones, he too senses doom: "Friends, we are but a red morning mist fleeting before a hot white sun. Red kills red while white multiplies." But he has a prophecy for the whites as well: "Friends, the time will come when the white man will wish he never saw the land of the red man. . . . When he thinks himself alone with his plow, suddenly, the spirit of the red man will rise out of the green grass underfoot and it will mourn at his elbow and it will cry for him not to destroy this beautiful land" (65).

Perhaps that time has come, and we sense the spirit of the red man at our elbow in the stench of our pollution of his land.

B. *"Lew and Luanne"*

Thurs, the hero of *Wanderlust*, is home in Siouxland working as hired hand for Lew between his freshman and sophomore years. He is teased for being a college boy, proves his worth, but doesn't seem the right boy for Luanne, Lew's daughter. The unattractive Art Donkers, another possible suitor, is driven off by Lew and his wife, who make him the butt of a practical joke. After Luanne's face is scarred in a bad car accident, for which Lew takes the minimum insurance payment, suitors do not come to her, and her father becomes increasingly protective. When she decides to marry the town mechanic, a man as old as Lew, trouble threatens, but father and daughter are soon reconciled.

In "Lew and Luanne," Manfred has paid tribute to his home community by depicting in Lew Lyons the personal traits that he admires most in the friends and neighbors of his youth; and in doing so, he has also shared with us that mix of backbreaking labor, antic good humor, and provincialism that are Siouxland characteristics.

Manfred, like Thurs, had to face some ridicule for going to college and having ambitions beyond the farm, yet he holds fast to the notion that farm boys are best prepared for life. In a recent interview, Manfred told a story about a pilot in World War II who insisted on having a navigator who was raised on the farm, because

farm boys always got in first where the others often got lost. He
quotes his pilot friend as saying, "I know when I get a boy from the
farm that if something happens up there, I'll have a fellow who . . .
is self reliant and can get home with the load. . . ."[28]

Lew sees Thurs as a "college bum" who doesn't have sense
enough to wear a hat in the sun. Rolf corrects him, saying, "He was
born and raised out here like the rest of us." But Lew isn't convinced. "Yeh, but the trouble is he's read a book," Lew complains
(74). Luanne wants Lew to hire Thurs, but Lew insists: "Naa. He'll
never be any good. He reads books. And goes to college" (88).

The truth may be, though, that Lew is jealous of Thurs, who in
front of Luanne proved himself to be a better worker than Lew in
spite of his reading and who is the first threat Lew has experienced
to a strong father-daughter relationship.

The contrast between country and city ways is explored again in
section three, when Bob Vincent, football star and successful insurance adjustor, comes from the Twin Cities to tame the terrible
"Lyon" who supposedly shoots insurance men. Bob expects to deal
with an inflated demand for damages and is unprepared for the individual integrity he finds in Lew, who takes only the bare amount
of expenses. "We don't believe in making a profit on what the Lord
wills. Goddurn it," Lew says (120). The local agent tries to explain
Lew to Bob: "He just sits tight on that little quarter section of land
and tries to live out his life quiet. Don't bother me and I won't
bother you, is his motto" (107). When Bob meets Lew, he sees him
as a "Lyon that is a lion," a rural aristocrat full of pride and confidence. When Luanne wants at least some "pride money," Lew
rears back: "Pride money? Since when has a Lyon growed a pride
that can be traded for money" (119).

Perhaps it is the Lyon pride that has enabled Lew to come
through so many disappointments and still have confidence and
good humor. He had wanted a boy, but he was denied other
children because of his wife's operation for cancer. He had grown to
love Luanne, only to have the accident destroy her beauty and opportunities for marriage. Because he would like another chance at
the world, his initial opposition to the man Luanne finally marries is
based more on jealousy than on personal feeling. "Bald is right.
He's balder than me," Lew exclaims. "But what you forget, Paw, is
that he ain't related," Luanne reminds her father. Lew would like
to be in Ray's place, starting out with a young wife like Luanne: "Is
this what I grew old for? . . . And him, that Ray, yet to begin?"
(144).

"Lew and Luanne" is billed as a comedy, and it satisfies on that score with its rustic characters and humor, its ridiculous situations, and its happy ending. Yet with all this fun, there is recognition of the serious tension that exists between "home folks" and the "city slickers" or the "college bums." Furthermore, had Luanne not been her father's "boy," she wouldn't have been able to face up to the ruin of her face and then choose for herself the man she needed. Luanne was able to "get home with the load" as a matter of course, being farm bred.

C. *"Country Love"*

In the third novelette, the love theme takes on a triangular aspect, with two boyhood pals, Ray and Jute, competing for Dolly. When Jute is blinded in a car accident, Ray feels responsible, since he was driving. The blind Jute gets moody and drinks, but encourages Ray and Dolly to marry. Finally, their son entices Jute on a fishing trip, and he resumes a productive life without self-pity.

Although the love of Ray and Jute for Dolly is important in the plot, it is the relationship between the boys that Manfred emphasizes in "Country Love." After their fight as ten year olds, they become "chums." Once Ray asked his father, "Dad, was you ever such good chums with a boy like I'm chums with Jute?" Ray's father cautions the boy: "Let's hope you and Jute will always remain good friends" (153). They do remain friends, in spite of Jute's blindness, Ray's guilt, and Dolly's love for both.

What they feel for each other may be close to what Walt Whitman calls "The institution of the dear love of comrades." In "The Prairie-Grass Dividing" Whitman writes:

The prairie-grass dividing, its special odor breathing,
I demand of it the spiritual corresponding,
Demand the most copious and close companionship of men,
Demand the blades to rise of words, acts, beings,
Those of the open atmosphere, coarse, sunlit, fresh, nutritious,

. . .

Those of earth-born passion, simple, never constrain'd, never obedient
Those of inland America.[29]

This companionship of men, Whitman feels, is to be desired above power and riches. These lines from "When I Peruse the Conquered Fame" suggest something of the relationship between Ray and Jute:

How together through life, through dangers, odium, unchanging, long and
long,
Through youth and through middle and old age, how unfaltering, how
affectionate and faithful they were,
Then I am pensive—I hastily walk away fill'd with the bitterest envy.[30]

It is this male affection that Ray would like to recapture if only Jute
would take some pride in himself. He knows a contented Jute would
make a good neighbor and thinks, "What could be more wonderful
than that a man was happy with his wife and kids, and then that his
best friend lived just across the way?" The minister reminds Jute of
the Bible story of David, and of Jonathan's death: "I am distressed
for thee, my brother Jonathan. Very pleasant hast thou been unto
me. Thy love to me was wonderful, passing the love of woman"
(195).

All three novelettes show Cupid's "arrow of love" striking unlike-
ly targets. In "Arrow of Love," the lovers are of enemy bands and
are doomed; in "Lew and Luanne," a father and daughter survive
through country grit and pride; and in "Country Love," two chums
learn through tragedy the power of manly love.

Of the stories in *Arrow of Love*, the title story is most impressive,
not only because it relates universal themes to Indian life, but also
because it has the same ring of authenticity that Manfred has been
able to bring to his Indian tales. "Lew and Luanne" and "Country
Love," while important in revealing different manifestations of the
love theme, are both too melodramatic and too laden with jocular
events which distract from the central motifs.

VII   Apples of Paradise *(1968)*

Between 1939 and 1967 Manfred wrote a number of stories
touching, in one way or another, the theme of childlessness. They
were collected in one volume and published in 1968 under the title
Apples of Paradise, the name of the second story in the collection.

If there is an attitude common to all the stories, it might be found
in these lines from "The Mink Coat" (1967), the lead story and the
most recently written: "The Hayden Foxxes were childless. On that
count everybody felt sorry for them."[31] After twelve years, both
Foxxes find themselves experimenting sexually with other partners.
Hayden is attracted to his secretary, and Miriam finds a lover when
she is stood up by her husband on a trip to an Arizona resort. The
story turns on a gift of a fur coat from her lover, which she tries to

hide from her husband. In an ironic twist, the coat winds up on the back of Hayden's secretary, and Miriam can't say a thing about it. Although childlessness provides some motivation for the sexual exploration, the basic interest is in plot and the buildup for a surprise ending.

In the title story, "Apples of Paradise," (1963), Manfred returns to a favorite theme in pitting the naturalness of sex against the artificiality of church dogma. The Renners, Ad and Sadie, are childless and are afraid to make love because their doctor has warned them of Sadie's delicate health, and their church has forbidden contraceptives. Their young boarder, Free, convinces Sadie that the church has no business interfering with the private lives of its members and persuades her to seduce her husband into love making. "I don't believe God has it in mind to forbid you that particular apple tree in the Garden of Eden," he tells her (96). Eventually, children are born and all is well. Their doctor had been a member of their church. Unhampered by dogma, the younger Free is able to lead the older couple into a paradise of natural behavior.

In "Wild Land" (1957), paradise is haunted. Jasper Dollarhide, a bachelor homesteader in Siouxland, involves himself with neighboring sisters, Lucy the quiet one and Delphine the playful one. He marries Lucy, but gives up in despair when no children are born. When Lucy plows up the "haunted" wild acres against the warnings of superstition, she dies of injuries she receives in working the land. Delphine, who has lived with the couple, takes Lucy's place and produces four children. The implication is that taming land intended to be wild is harmful, just as taming free nature causes sterility in Lucy. The "wilder," more playful Delphine is productive.

In "Blood Will Tell" (1954), a post-Civil War story, the wilderness runs unchecked in Ira Barber, who lives with Dawn Breaking, a halfbreed, and beats her. Doc Chalmers patches her up each time and makes Ira jealous. After a snake bite and a punch in the nose, Ira is tamed. When he learns that he, too, is a "breed," son of Captain Clark's black servant and a Yankton Sioux, he no longer feels superior to Dawn and wants to marry her in the Indian way. "There ain't a man living on God's green earth what he ain't some kind of breed or other," Doc tells Ira (156). Childlessness, as such, is not a factor in the story, but the new healthy relationship between Ira and Dawn is one which can produce children unashamed of their mixed blood.

The goodhearted man in "Goodhearted Man" (1953) is Crimp Wickett of Bonnie, Siouxland, a humpnecked fiddler and square dance caller who, at forty, achieves national prominence. With his six daughters married and his wife dead, he is lonely and yet surprised when he finds himself making a pass, innocently he thinks, at his too attractive piano player. "Well, that's men for you," he thinks in embarrassment as he heads for his empty house (181). The childless theme is given a subtle twist here. Crimp has had six daughters, but they have married and left him childless again. In Hulda, the pretty piano player, he sees a "sister-in-arms" of his dead wife and responds to her instinctively, goodheartedly. Yet the girl, already "damaged" by her uncommon attractiveness to men, sees Crimp as just another dirty old man. "What? You too?" she asks as she runs from him.

In "Treehouse" (1951), it is size that frustrates and prevents children. Mathew and Hermina Haugen are Jack Spratt and his wife. She is huge and Matt is scrubby, but a "hardy scrub exactly because he's living on a fine root system started early in youth" (187). Living with Hermina is to Matt like living in a treehouse in the shade of maple leaves. They like each other but are childless, even though Matt is "a regular little bull of a man." Tired of Duluth snow, Matt gives up his harbor master job so they can travel south with a house trailer. They try Florida and the Southwest but stop at the California redwoods, which fascinate Matt. He buys a motel built around a tree, but Hermina is not happy. Matt likes the humbling perspective the huge trees give, making him feel like he has been to church and had his life changed. "What is man compared to these giants in the earth?" he asks. When Hermina threatens to cut their tree down, Matt pretends a love affair with a pretty tourist and wins her back. The story is a strange mixture of serious speculation about the human condition and incongruous, almost vaudevillian humor.

"High Tenor" (1951) presents another kind of frustration, that of homosexuality, which prevents marriage and the birth of children. Timothy Stor, tenor, and Magdalena van Dellen, organist, are attracted to each other and marry, but after eight days the marriage has not been consummated, and Tim, finally confronted by Magdalena's golden naked body, runs out into the night. Ironically, Tim first senses his love for Magdalena during his singing of the tenor solo in the "Messiah," with such words as, "The crooked straight and the rough places plain," and "Behold and see if there be any sorrow like unto His sorrow. He was cut off out of the land of the living" (222).

The sexual exuberance of "Boys Will Be Boys" (1946) provides a contrast to the sexual inhibition of "High Tenor," yet both stories reflect unfulfilled lives. While waiting for their father to arrive with his new bride, grown sons Archy and Rich exchange tales of their sexual exploits, only to discover that their father's new bride is a girl both have "had" and have been joking about. A normal love relationship is as impossible for Archy and Rich as it is for Tim in "High Tenor." Rich tells Archy, "Sometimes you act as if you almost hate women." And Archy passes it off by saying, "Just haven't found the right one yet. One that can cook and shut up both" (245). They, too, may remain childless.

The mysteries of birth and death are explored in "Footsteps in the Alfalfa" (1939), as Frank Bramstad and his wife Laura try to make enough out of farming to pay the rent. It is spring and a time for new beginnings, and as Frank works to help his favorite cow give birth, he has a queer feeling that all is not well. He has a ringing in his ears, for one thing, and then when his cow dies he sees that as a bad omen. He tries to put superstition behind him, and reasons, "The real thing to do was to work hard, to do one's best, and then to just sit back and wait—and wonder if it would be the earth's pleasure to come up with a crop" (265). Having this attitude, Frank is able to accept his childlessness and to appreciate his wife for the loving woman that she is. "There is no doubt about it," he thinks. "Laura was a fine helpmate. A fine good woman. And it was his duty, as a good husband, to overlook those times she got mad because she still didn't have a baby. Laura wasn't much different from the earth. Sometimes the earth got mad too" (267). The cyclical pattern of good and bad spins several times for Frank that day. The cow dies, but he finds an unexpected calf in the field; the dog saves him from a bull, but the dog is injured in the reaper and must be killed; there is no money for the rent, but somehow the owner gives him more time. He senses the mystery about him in the earth as a strange ringing in his ears, a whisper of footsteps in the alfalfa. Laura tells him it is his guilty conscience, but he isn't convinced.

"Footsteps in the Alfalfa" is an appropriate conclusion to the volume, for it puts childlessness in its proper perspective as one of the possibilities in life that must be endured. "Having babies has its dark side too" (265), Frank discovers in the death of his cow. The setting lets Manfred report movingly on the rural life he knows best. His descriptions of the birth of a calf and of cutting alfalfa are dramatically real, and Manfred's artistry comes in using those details to evoke awareness of the human condition.

Another strong story in the volume is "The Wild Land," which achieves the ring of authenticity while defining a mystical connection between the land and human personality. Much weaker stories are "Mink Coat," most recently written (1967), and "Boys Will Be Boys." "Mink Coat" is superficial and seems contrived for the sake of its surprise ending. "Boys Will Be Boys" is simply an example of ironical country humor.

In general, Manfred's stories reflect his deft touch with narrative and his sure ear for dialogue. As one event is piled upon another, these show the paradoxical nature of human beings as creators and destroyers, courageous in their suffering and loyal to their dreams of love.

VIII   Winter Court (1966)

In 1966, Manfred collected the poems he had written between 1934 and 1965 and organized them chronologically under the title of the longest poem, "Winter Count." The slim, handsomely bound first edition was limited to a thousand copies.

Although there are no groupings of the poems, they naturally cluster around four places: those written at Calvin College, Grand Rapids, Michigan, and on the way to and from that school (1934 - 1937); those written at Oak Terrace, Minnesota, during the two years he was a patient in the tuberculosis sanatorium there (1940 - 1942); those written at Wrâlda, his home in Bloomington, Minnesota, overlooking the Minnesota River valley (1948 - 1956); and those written at Blue Mound, Luverne, Minnesota (1961 - 1965).

In the four hundred and seventy-four lines of the poem "Winter Count," Manfred imitates the Indian historian by marking off the first eighteen winters of his life. Using free verse and a narrative style, he details particular events to represent his early years on farms near Doon, Iowa. The technique is not unlike that he uses in the Buckskin Man Tales, where he selects particular years out of nineteenth century Siouxland as keys to the nature of that period.

The events he selects to record range from the humorous through the bittersweet to the tragic. There are childhood memories of taking care of his four brothers, of starting school, teasing his teacher, being punished, and being caught in a blizzard. There are the high school years paid for by milking cows, the ball games, the summer farm work. There is, at seventeen, his mother's death, sketched in so few lines, but etched into the reader's mind with homely details—the two year old in the crib showing his dead mother his teddy bear, asking for a cookie; the father and son bumping into each other as they hurry to enter the door together but too late. Then, at eighteen, another important moment is recorded, when his father announces marriage to the housekeeper, and the poet realizes he is free to go to college.

> Free to go to college
> Provided I worked my way through
> But free
> Eighteen winters and free.[32]

"Free" is the name Manfred has given to a character in recent stories who, he says, resembles him more than any other of his created people.

Ironically, in chronological order following "Winter Count," where the young man is free to begin his adult life, there is a poem, "I Am Fifty," in which the poet feels his life is done, misspent; however, that is followed in turn by "Boiling Rock," in which a kind of rebirth occurs, as the writer is lying naked on a rock that seems to be "some fundamental rib of the earth." "I feel an old heat rising out of the rock. It fires my young arteries and my young heart" (76).

In "Boiling Rock," Manfred touches a theme he develops in several novels, the need to return for guidance and renewal to the "old ones," to the primordial knowledges we have neglected. Both the first poem in the volume, dated July 1934, and the last one, of July 3, 1965, concern this respect for origins. In "The West Sends a Call," which opens the book, the poet lists items associated with farming and concludes, "all of these, have an appeal and a message that are pleasing to the primitive nature of man" (11). In the final poem, "Sioux Quartzite Smooth as Doves," Manfred describes another rock he loves to rest on to feel the spirit of the past:

> I fancy I can feel the lichen moving,
> an inch a minute on my skin. Improving.
> I feel warm lips upon my nose.

> I smell pink a wild rose.
> I hear a red man trilling in my head.
> I'll sing a song before I'm dead. (78)

However, the poem that most clearly shows the poet to be infused with the spirit of past times is "Medicine Wheel." After climbing high on a mountain to view the ancient design in the earth, he has a vision in which the sacrificial ceremonies are being acted out. So real is it that he gasps for breath and drives quickly to where it's flat.

In "Rapture of the Deeps," Manfred again shows identification with nature and a primordial past through dream. The poem moves from dreams of childhood into a kind of evolutionary nightmare out of which the following lines suggest a oneness man shares with the universe:

> I am neither above nor below
> But beside and among the dancing green deeps
> I am neither for nor against
> But of and by and with the dancing green sleeps. (49)

Another important Manfred theme that gets unique expression in the poems is male-female interrelationships, especially in "Four Voices in a Dream," written in 1952. Nevertheless, it is a key to understanding Manfred's two recent books: *Milk of Wolves* and *The Manly-Hearted Woman*. Both are concerned with the identification of male and female roles in society.

Keen sensitivity to human relationships is shown in the four "Maryanna" poems, written to his wife, and in "The Old Black Silence," a conversation with the poet's dying uncle. The poignant expressions of human love by the uncle are separated by metaphysical refrains which express man's loneliness in the universe: "There's little sign of Voice, / There's little sign of Choice" (58).

The forty-one poems in *Winter Count* are important for Manfred scholars, for they reveal something of the soul of the artist not so easily discerned in the novels, which are more valid as "art" than are the poems. In the poems, the ego is seen to be tamed at times with doubt; and the youthful exhilaration with freedom balanced with a dignified respect for uncles and aunts and family traditions.

Manfred's stories and poems alike seem to be either spinoffs from the novels or practice strokes in preparation for his more important and longer fictions. The poem "Winter Count," for example, provides a perfect outline to his recent autobiographical novel *Green Earth*. The poems entitled "Mother" and "Father" will have special meaning, too, for those who read that book. Manfred's poetry is personal in nature and will never be widely read, but the poetic impulse is strong in him, erupting in his prose passages as unique figures of speech and powerful word inventions. Perhaps his most significant poetic expression is in the language patterns and rhythms he created to represent the ancient tongues of Siouxland.

CHAPTER 5

Coming to Terms with The Old Lizard

ALTHOUGH the themes important to Manfred have been identified and described in the preceding chapters, the full reach of his artistic purpose can best be seen when the themes are examined in relationship to his total work. Not only is mysticism important as a theme running through all of Manfred's work, but it is also a key to his creative style and energy. A second major theme, that of bonding, centers around human relationships in their wonderful variety. The historical and philosophical perspectives out of which these themes arise show Manfred to be at the center of a developing tradition, identified by Max Westbrook as Western realism, which is centered on a concept he calls "sacrality."[1]

I *Mysticism*

Manfred's philosophy as well as his creative energy arise out of what is essentially a mystical understanding of the world—that is, he senses that spiritual truth or ultimate reality can be attained through subjective experience related to intuition or insight. His mysticism is especially keen as it relates to nature, to the land, to what D. H. Lawrence has termed the "spirit of place." It is this spirit which permeates the major conflicts in his work between the civilized and the primitive, the sophisticated and the natural, the superficial or hypocritical and the essential. Furthermore, Manfred sees his own creative energy as deriving ultimately from the sun, or from primordial sources he sometimes identifies as the "Old Lizard" or the "Old Adam." Contact with these sources is often made through dreams, which are taken seriously by Manfred in the process of writing and which figure importantly in the lives of many of his fictional characters. Similarly, the ancient myths are used in

140

developing the archetypal imagery which connects these modern works with the primordial. John Milton has referred to this characteristic in Manfred's writing as "the long view," seeing man in his proper relationship to the whole social history.

A. *Spirit of Place*

In the introductory chapter to *Studies in Classic American Literature*, D. H. Lawrence establishes his concept of the spirit of place:

Every continent has its own great spirit of place. Every people is polarized in some particular locality, which is home, the homeland. Different places on the face of the earth have different vital effluence, different vibration, different chemical exhalation, different polarity with different stars; call it what you like. But the spirit of place is a great reality.[2]

Lawrence goes on to infuse this spirit, this "it," with mystical power and says, "If one wants to be free, one has to give up the illusion of doing what one likes, and seek what 'it' wishes done." He suggests that, even as the migrating birds, we are brought to our goals by some invisible magnetism.

We are not the marvelous choosers and deciders we think we are. It chooses for us, and decides for us. Unless, of course, we are just escaped slaves, vulgarly cocksure of our ready-made destiny. But if we are living people, in touch with the source, IT drives us and decides us. We are free only so long as we obey. When we run counter, and think we will do as we like, we just flee around like Orestes pursued by the Eumenides.[3]

Manfred has enlarged upon this idea by suggesting that the "place" chooses us. Siouxland chose him, even though he gave it a name. We are so close to "It" that we are not used to thinking of what place means to us or of how, "in a casual chaotic way," it makes choices. The idea is essentially Greek. Edith Hamilton points out that the ancient Greeks did not believe that the gods created the universe, but rather that the universe created the gods. Heaven and earth were the first parents.

In a taped lecture, Manfred tells of a colleague of his who welcomed a winter blizzard in South Dakota because, as he said, "It will pinch out those who can't take it."[4] People, animals, and plants are "chosen" in this sense. Imagining what the "place" might think, Manfred has its spirit verbalize as follows: "You're going to be my voice eventually; I'm going to keep two thousand of you here, and among those, one of you will be a poet or sage or oracle, and I'll get said what I want to get said."[5]

Manfred feels that writers, artists, and composers create by listening for their individual "tone" as it is generated out of a place. Thus, he suggests that Faulkner would not be Faulkner apart from Mississippi, nor Manfred Manfred apart from Siouxland. The relationship is essentially mystical, subjective. Manfred tells his students: "Find that tone and no one can destroy you. You will have real power." Finding it, he says, is a matter of listening in solitude.[6]

Manfred has come to like the word "tone" better than "voice" in defining an author's unique way of expressing himself. Don Bebeau has pointed out that Manfred in his first book, *The Golden Bowl*, reached for and found his personal voice or tone, much as his hero Maury Grant came home to find his roots on the prairie farm he at first rejected. A central image in the book is of a worm at the end of a blade of grass reaching out for another blade so that it can go down again to the grass roots. Rootedness is important to Manfred. He says that his most important discovery as a novelist was that all great writers are regionalists. Once a writer can find a sense of place, he can find the appropriate tone.[7] It isn't just novelists who need this identification with place, but each individual, to be complete, needs to "evolve his own soul," as Manfred puts it:

I feel very strongly that there is something going on in the relationship of the human being to his environment. Eventually it makes his soul. I think you're given the nervous equipment to have a soul; that's all you're given at birth. After that your environment makes you whatever you are, makes your soul. And I think that we're beginning to have our soul out here.[8]

In this way, the connection between "tone" and "place" is basically religious, and an author's territory becomes sacred to him. Manfred feels that way about his home on Blue Mound in southwestern Minnesota. He has learned from geologists that the Sioux quartzite that makes up the Mounds is three and a half billion years old, formed at a time when there was no life on earth. The mounds were part of a mountain range that ran from Mitchell, South Dakota, to Mankato, Minnesota, and was higher than Mt. Everest. "Even when I was young, I was aware that this was a

special and odd place," he says. He reports that his friend, Frank
Waters, the novelist, picked up the tone of the place on his first
visit. Waters and Manfred had walked out over the top of the
mounds, with Waters maintaining a silence strange for him. Finally,
as Waters was leaving he said, "Listen, Fred, you built your house
on a sacred place. You'd better live right here. . . . this is a sacred
place and don't offend it."[9]

B.   *The Old Lizard*

One way to understand what Manfred means when he speaks of
the "Old Lizard" or the "Old Leviathan" or the "Old Adam" is to
think of the way in which time and glaciers have worn down the tall
Minnesota mountain range to mere mounds and prairies. In people,
civilization has had the effect of wearing away the primordial
knowledge that was once more easily accessible to us. Manfred says:
"Our civilization, and all the other levels of nations we have gone
through, and all the things we've learned to do by reason and
because of common sense, have gradually wiped out our most
powerful ally. And that is our primate nature. What I call the Old
Lizard. Or the Old Leviathan."[10] The lizard is more than just the
subconscious, according to Manfred; it is akin to instinct or to C. G.
Jung's notion of the collective unconscious. A biologist might call it
"molecular memory." As a race, we have lost touch with primordial
wisdom, perhaps in the same way we as adults have lost the childlike ability to react openly to a situation, free of inhibition. "The
Old Adam is still alive in the child," as Manfred says. "The Old
Primate still hangs around in us. If you get him on your side as a
writer you have got it."[11]

One of the ways to get him on your side, Manfred contends, is to
pay attention to dreams. "I've dreamed all the characters in every
one of my books." He recalls awakening one night on the margin
between dream and reality to Thurs Wraldson standing at the foot
of his bed, hero of his *Wanderlust* trilogy. Another time while walking he thought he saw Thurs coming toward him on the road. During the writing of *Scarlet Plume*, he dreamed on several occasions of
a white girl and an Indian.[12]

The more books Manfred writes, the better he gets at dreaming
and at using dreams as a stimulus to imagination. He feels that ex-
pert writers learn how to use "that side of yourself that is for fan-
tasies." He is familiar with Freud's *Interpretation of Dreams*, but

disagrees with about two-thirds of it on the grounds that Freud sees everything from today's prejudices, rather than from the early primate's point of view.

C. *Usable Past*

To get that other point of view, to find a usable past against which he could project his more modern heroes, Manfred turned to the writing of the Buckskin Man Tales. He had the mystical notion that the "ghosts of the old boys," the spirits of the people who once inhabited Siouxland, were "in the air" somehow. Walt Whitman expressed it this way in "Passage to India":

> The past—the dark unfathomed retrospect!
> The teaming gulf—the sleepers and the shadows!
> The past—the infinite greatness of the past!
> For what is the present after all but a growth out of the past?[13]

Just as in *Conquering Horse*, No Name turns to his wakan white stallion as a great father and teacher, so in the Buckskin Man Tales, Manfred returns to the Indian culture of the prairies to show us how the Indian got his "soul" through an interrelationship with his environment—with animal, bird, and insect as well as with the elements and with growing things.

An examination of the mystical elements in the five tales will show what Manfred means when he says that civilization has worn away primordial knowledges and denied us an orientation toward nature that our modern world desperately needs, especially now as natural resources disappear. As the white culture gradually wears away the native Indian mode of life, the role of the mystical is consciously suppressed.

The characteristics of the mystical experience are consistent throughout the five tales. Always highly personal, the event takes the form of a union with nature, an ability to communicate with the animal kingdom and to draw power from the elements of nature. Ultimately, the union was not only with nature but with the course of events in the form of prophetic vision, as with *Conquering Horse*.

The mystical experience is at the center of the Indian culture in *Conquering Horse*, which is set before any white people had arrived. Without a vision to guide him, No Name was nothing; therefore, he consciously tried to achieve union with the six powers by fasting and undergoing physical torture.

In contrast to this willed vision, Hugh Glass in *Lord Grizzly* has a vision accidentally and doesn't recognize what has happened to him. He is forced into fasting and physical torture in order to survive, and thus he forges a link to the animal world which protects him and gives him energy. From the moment he fights the grizzly, Hugh becomes more and more like the grizzly. He wears the bear's hide, uses its claws, eats its rotting meat, and lives. Another bear licks maggots from his wounds, and eventually on the White river he has a mystical vision of a grizzly following him. After this, his hair turns grizzly white, and this experience contributes to his eventual decision to forgive Jim and Fitz, for he finds that they too have had a struggle for survival as rigorous as his own. There is a bonding between Hugh and his boys that is stronger than any desire for revenge, which was dictated by a mere human code. In the end, Hugh remains confused by his accidental mystical adventure and says, "Turned tame, this child has. Passed through such a passel of things he don't rightly recollect wrong from right no more" (281).

Where Hugh Glass achieved his mystical experience in a struggle for life, Scarlet Plume's conscious mysticism led him to accept death. Although the nature of Scarlet Plume's vision is never explained, clearly it was similar to that of No Name and of Flat Warclub in *The Manly-Hearted Woman*. He achieves a mystical attitude of acceptance toward death and rises above the degrading circumstances surrounding his final hours. Judith is inspired by his behavior and leaves the white community to try and discover what he had found.

Blue Swallow in *King of Spades* also escapes the white culture in an effort to retain a mystical union with nature. She blends into the forest and can communicate with the animals. Like Hugh Glass, she had to develop this ability in order to survive alone in the Edenlike forest. But she is a white girl Indian trained and cannot live in a civilization which rapes the land, fells the trees, and slaughters the animals. Ransom loses her, as we have lost what she represents, because he lusts for gold. He cannot have a mystical union with nature and destroy it at the same time.

The mystical talent has virtually disappeared in *Riders of Judgement*, along with the Indians. Whites are fighting whites in a range war. Some little evidence of the mystical remains, however, in Cain Hammett. He has a strange ability to communicate with animals, and he senses in himself an equally strange power to control others. He is uncomfortable with such power, however, and suppresses it for fear of hurting someone. Only as he is facing death does he feel free to let his "animal" out full force. Civilized man is embarrassed by mystical powers and fears that they may be evil. Thus the mystical is forced underground, as the old mountains were pushed into the plains. The mountains may be underneath, as the Blue Mounds give the sign, and the Old Lizard may still be in us all, but the signs are hard to read. Manfred is trying to interpret for us.[14]

In *The Man Who Killed the Deer*, Frank Waters has Byers, a white man friendly to the Pueblo Indians, speculate on why this instinctive, intuitive, nonreasoning approach to life is disappearing, even though "by infallible instinct and undivided consciousness the Indian has proved the validity of his approach." Byers concludes that "because he couldn't or wouldn't express it articulately, the whole shebang was passing with him." By "shebang," Byers means "the magnificent surrender of self to the unseen forces whose instruments we are, and the fulfillment of whose purposes gives us our only meaning."[15]

Perhaps it is impossible to express this wordless faith articulately without the natural symbolism of ceremonials and dance dramas, but at least Manfred is trying. Furthermore, in his articulation of these primitive ways of knowing, he is at the same time leading us toward a "transformation of consciousness" which the modern world desperately needs. As a novelist, he uses the past to bring us to new worlds.

The main argument of Anton Zijderveld, in *The Abstract Society*, is that modern man, because he has placed himself outside the meanings of social life, has reduced his nature to that of a conditioned animal or of an infant who is unable to act adequately if changes in his environment occur. He is a conformist who submits to the unexpected, or he is a protester who often appears to be aimless. Zijderveld distinguishes modern abstract, pluralistic society from so-called primitive or developing societies and suggests that modern industrial man is not the "normal" one, but a deviation from what the Dutch historian Jan Romein labels the "Common Human Pattern (CHP)". The CHP man is defined as follows:

He has a subjective attitude toward nature. He feels himself part of nature and thus cannot objectify it. This has implications for his attitude toward science and technology, both of which try to manipulate nature in an objective, value-free way. The CHP-man rather endures nature. His magic, I might add, is a form of manipulation, but it is a manipulation of powers that are inherent to nature and cannot be understood through objective knowledge. Moreover, he has no free access to nature since this is barred by countless taboos. His conception of life is part of a cosmic philosophy. That is, life is not something that happens to you, and since outside this world nothing can exist, death is seen as only a transition to a different mode of existence.[16]

Such a man is not abstract; he is concrete and pragmatic. Zijderveld believes the theory of the Common Human Pattern has a heuristic value for modern society. Today, estranged from nature, man endures his society as something that confronts him, not as something he lives and is a part of. On the contrary, the CHP man is tightly integrated with his social collectivity (clan, tribe) and even sees nature as part of the unit. Zijderveld writes: "These ties between man and his environment, strong as they were in the Common Human Pattern, have been severed in the process of modernization. The individual has become autonomous and so has his social environment."[17]

In comparing the present abstract society with the CHP, Zijderveld is not calling for a return to the primitive but rather for a humanization of modern society. He says this requires a new form of consciousness, through which man can regain control over the process of segmentation that has affected his life and mind in the form of specialization and professionalism. Through this new consciousness he must learn to control his emotionality and find a balance between rationality and irrationality.[18] Zijderveld calls for an attitude of "intellectual asceticism" in the reform of consciousness.

In an essay for the *Saturday Review*, the novelist Joyce Carol Oates likewise asks for a new consciousness, for a meticulous genius like Kant "to synthesize vast exploratory fields of knowledge, to write the book that is the way into the future for us . . . one that will climb up out of the categories of 'rational' and 'irrational' to show why the consciousness of the future will feel joy not dread at . . . the absorption into the psychic stream of the universe." In the meantime, Oates looks to both science and literature for help in breaking down old assumptions and preparing the way for the new world of "higher humanism or pantheism." She quotes the British physicist-philosopher Sir James Jeans, as follows:

Today there is a wide measure of agreement, which on the physical side of science approaches almost to unanimity, that the stream of knowledge is heading toward a non-mechanical reality; the universe begins to look more like a great thought than like a great machine. Mind no longer appears as an accidental intruder into the realm of matter; we are beginning to suspect that we ought rather to hail it as the creator and governor of the realm of matter. . . .[19]

From the novelists she wants "an absolutely honest literature . . . to dramatize for us the complexities of this epoch, showing us how deeply related we are to one another, how deeply we act out, even in our apparently secret dreams, the communal crises of our world."[20]

Long before Joyce Carol Oates issued this call, Manfred had identified his role as a novelist in similar terms: "In my work I want to be a voice speaking—telling how we are and how we were; that is, how we grew up and these were our dreams and, too bad, we are going to die. This is holy work. I'm in it for keeps."[21]

II   *Bonding*

In "telling how we are and how we were" and how deeply related we are to one another, Manfred explores in all of his novels the theme of human bonding. He is interested in male and female relationships and roles, under both normal and abnormal circumstances, as a way of showing us to ourselves. The pervasiveness of the bonding theme in Manfred's work may be seen if some of the human relationships in his books are listed under bonding categories identified by Lionel Tiger and Robin Fox in *The Imperial Animal* and in Tiger's *Men in Groups*. The categories would be male to female, mother to child, father to child, and male to male.

A.   *Male to Female Bond*

In the evolutionary process, a true social system begins when animals respond differentially to other members of the species as individuals and begin to select other members for permanent interaction, usually as a means of defending territory. The male usually defends the territory, but in order to reproduce he must be joined by a female. These mates are attached to each other and work together to protect their young and feed each other, but there is always the potential of aggression between them. The male is initially hostile to all intruders, but in order to mate, he has had to come to terms with his female partner. This love and hate are built into the very nature of the bonding process, according to Tiger and

Fox. Unless there is something to force the individuals apart, there is no reason to evolve a complicated means of bringing them together. Out of this paradox, Tiger and Fox identify the following biological principle: "The more highly developed the species, the more likely there is to be a high degree of individualism and aggressiveness, and hence of mistrust, and consequently of bonding."[22]

The many male to female bonds Manfred writes of show a variability of response that Tiger and Fox see as typical, as compared to the invariability of the mother to child bond. In *This is the Year*, Pier's stubborn defense of his territory dominates his relationship with his wife Nertha. He neglects or is ignorant of the ritual grooming activities necessary to set up a perfect bond, and as a result he loses both his wife and his territory. With proper attention paid to these grooming activities, which tend to reduce male aggression toward the female, even extreme cultural differences will not break the bond, as illustrated in that between Scarlet Plume and Judith in *Scarlet Plume* or between the Stoneboilers in *Milk of Wolves*.

In contrast to Pier's neglect of sex for territory, Garrett Engleking, in *The Man Who Looked Like the Prince of Wales*, sacrifices territory for sex. The ritual grooming was all. However, the bond can hold virtually without sex, as indicated in *Eden Prairie*, where Kon and Karen are more like brother and sister than man and wife. Sex isn't the only ritual important in male to female bonding.

B. *Mother to Child Bond*

Even more fundamental than the "pair" bond, according to Tiger and Fox, is the bond between mother and child. It is especially important in the human species because man is the "supermammal":

This means that he exaggerates the behavioral characteristics—an increase in learning ability dependent on the greater size and complexity of the brain, and even more pronounced period of mother-child dependency, a greater emotional ability, a more elaborate sexuality, more complex play, more spectacular aggressivity, a greater propensity for bonding, a more extended system of communications, and so on.[23]

While it is true that the mammalian mother has to suckle the child, Tiger and Fox point out that the higher we mount on the scale of mammalian complexity, the more evident it is that something other than simple feeding is involved in the mother-child relationship. That something is the basic learning which comes during the suckling period and which contributes to emotional security. Tiger and Fox write: "Simply on the basis of what we know about the social mammals in general, we can predict that if the mother-child bond does not go right, the unfortunate youngster may never get any of his other bonds right."[24] Just as the mother is totally essential to the early well-being of her offspring, so her separation from the child is necessary for its later well-being. It begins with the physiological act of weaning and ends with the transference of emotional ties to peers and mates.

In *Morning Red*, Manfred shows the difficulties which arise when a mother fails to terminate her bond. Jack Nagel is "bent" and prevented from having satisfactory bonds in later life, Manfred suggests, because his mother was overprotective, as symbolized in Jack's excessive thumb sucking. Likewise, Elizabeth's problems about sex seemed to stem from negative attitudes learned early and well from her mother. These prevented her satisfactory bonding as an adult.

The proper attitude for a mother to take is illustrated in Manfred's Indian tales, where the Yanktons treat the mother's breast as sacred but at the same time honor the mother who knows when to let her child go. In *Conquering Horse*, No Name tells his wife, "My mother told me a great thing when I was about to depart. 'Son, the thing you seek lives in a far place. It is good. Go to it. Do not turn around after you have gone part way, but go as far as you were going and then come back.' " Leaf answers, "When I am old, may it be given me to say such a thing to my son" (247).

In *King of Spades*, the male protectiveness of Magnus combines with female overprotectiveness of the son to generate violence. Both the male-female and the mother-child bonds are skewed, and the result is tragic. Tragedy can result also when no child results from a marriage bond, as shown in the stories grouped together in *Apples of Paradise*.

C.   Brother to Sister Bond

Tiger and Fox point out that a parental bond in the human species need not be between sexual partners. Once the female is impregnated, asexual blood bonds such as between brother and sister or between cousins are often more stable than the more loosely knit bond between husband and wife.[25]

In *Milk of Wolves*, Manfred shows us a strong brother-sister bond between Flur and Faunce. In this instance, the competition between a blood tie and a mating tie resulted in tragedy. If Juhl had been killed rather than Flur, Faunce and Flur might have been ideal parents for the baby. As things turned out, though, Juhl was left alone and had to serve as mother, even to the extent of suckling the child. In *Morning Red*, Liz and Lilibet are so closely associated in the mind of Walt, who is Liz's brother and Lilibet's husband, that he gives them a common name. There is even a hint that he may have taken his sister's virginity.

Blood ties in *Riders of Judgement*, though not brother and sister, are important to the theme of the book. Three brothers express love toward a cousin, with the true parentage of the child in doubt and somehow unimportant. There is a traditional fear of such a bond between cousins because it might increase an "outlaw" streak in the family line. On the other hand, such a bond could improve the family if the "streak" were positive.

D. *Father to Child Bond*

In writing about the "male sweetness of life," Manfred is particularly interested in males and the conflicting roles men play as lovers, husbands, and fathers. The father role is most carefully expressed in *Conquering Horse*, where No Name as a new father learns his role by watching the stallion Dancing Sun protect and manage his herd. The lover role is best exemplified in *Scarlet Plume*, where Manfred presents his Indian hero as "the male at his height, at his most fulfilled moment." Scarlet Plume as lover is much more to be admired than Judith's neglectful husband, who deserts his family and prefers unorthodox sex. He does not understand the significance of ritual grooming to making a successful bond.

The ideal husband, on the other hand, is seen in the Indian Wulf Stoneboiler in *Milk of Wolves*, for he sacrifices himself for his wife. The least successful husband and father would be Dad Nagel in *Morning Red*, for he tries to mold his son Jack into his own image and to force him into the family business. Tiger and Fox explain the difficulty in such a situation by pointing out that "a father and son who have a complex history of support and authority will be tried by the equality necessary to run a business together." One bond tends to make a second bond difficult, they point out.[26]

An opposite view of the father-son relationship is seen in circumstances where the son tries to replace the father, either as head of the group or as lover. The father who fears the son is like Cronos in the Greek myth, who tries to drown his sons because he has been told that one will replace him. The most striking example of such a circumstance is in *King of Spades*, where Magnus King's unnatural fear results in tragedy. The Cronos theme is seen more poignantly in *Conquering Horse* as No Name reluctantly moves, at the command of his vision, to kill and replace his father as leader of the tribe. In *This is the Year*, Pier brutally forces his parents off the home place, and in *Eden Prairie*, Charlie tries to do the same with his father, Anse.

The father-daughter bond, according to Tiger and Fox, is the most common incestuous encounter, but it is not common in Manfred's plots. Incest of any kind, they point out, is not common because to commit it one must "disrupt an already established bond and substitute another and often antipathetical one. . . . In terms of central tendency, most people do not commit incest, most men are unfaithful, and most people who have had a superordinate-subordinate relationship do not easily convert it to a bond of equality."[27]

E. *Male to Male Bond*

In his book *Men in Groups*, Lionel Tiger suggests that the biological need for male bonding may be as universal as the need for sex, food, shelter, and social interaction. In primate societies the male bond, with its initiation ceremonies, reflects a "pattern of unisexual selection for work, defense, and hunting purposes comparable to sexual selection for reproductive ones." Tiger points out, furthermore, that aggressive behavior is "a function and/or outgrowth of corporate male interaction."[28] Such aggression in the past has stimulated creativity in men and has enabled them to protect their women and families as well as to provide food. In the modern world, with its sophisticated weapons system, aggression can be counterproductive and destroy all societies. The problem, as Lionel Tiger sees it, is in knowing how to slow down aggression by weakening male bonding structures without at the same time hindering males from achieving creative stimulus and a satisfactory individual experience.[29]

In hunting and warrior societies, such as those represented by the Indians Manfred writes of in *Conquering Horse, Scarlet Plume, The Manly-Hearted Woman*, and *Arrow of Love*, the male bond is often more important than the male-female bond. Tiger and Fox describe, for example, a Crow Indian ritual in which each brave before a battle tells the group about his lovers since the last raid, even though names of wives and daughters are recited. The slate is wiped clean; the warrior band is freed from contamination by sexual jealousy and can go about its essentially male business of fighting the enemy.

In *The Manly-Hearted Woman*, a similar ceremony takes place when Flat Warclub is given permission to have any woman he wants before he dies in battle. This was the sign of ultimate acceptance into the male group, an acceptance that had been denied Flat Warclub until his vision of death. Once accepted, he was able to prove his manliness, whereas without the male bond he doubted his own capacity to be fully a man.

In the settlement of the West, male bonding was an important factor. Hugh Glass in *Lord Grizzly* felt that the "mountain man code" had been broken when Fitz and Jim left him to die alone. He learns to forgive them, eventually, because he sees that he too broke the bond when he went hunting alone against orders.

Tiger and Fox point out that when faced with danger, men go to extreme lengths to reaffirm the male to male bond at the expense of the male to female. In *Riders of Judgment*, although the main fight is between the big as opposed to the little cattle operators, the most vicious punishment is given to "Cattle Kate," who presumed to use her female charms in building a herd. In *King of Spades*, Ransom gives up his idyllic bond with Erden in favor of the male group of miners and gold, the symbol of male power and control.

The need for male grouping is explored also in *Milk of Wolves*, when Juhl leaves his unsatisfactory family situation to join an all male lumbering outfit. As in the case of Flat Warclub, Juhl had just been rejected by the army as being "unstable," an "artist," and needed to prove his manliness as a "man among men." He volunteers for the dangerous job of topping a tree. Although Juhl had failed as a husband and father, he had proven his male capacity as a lover and creator. Nevertheless, there was a biological need in his life for male bonding, which the lumbercamp provided and which led to another spurt of creative energy. In a more modern setting, the political groups in *Morning Red* illustrate the way men use male to male bonds in organizing themselves to gain power.

III   Historical and Philosophical Perspectives

Frederick Manfred's work cannot be forced into conformation with any particular literary theory or mode. He writes from historical perspectives, but he is not an historical novelist nor a "Western" writer; he writes about the world as he senses it, and his perspective reflects a full range of attitudes, from the realistic to the naturalistic to the existential and to the sacred. He might not object to being called a regionalist, but only if the Siouxland region is seen as a doorway to universals. He prefers to be known as a storyteller, much as Juhl in *Milk of Wolves* wants to be known as a stonecutter rather than as a sculptor.

A.   Historical

The Buckskin Man Tales are the most historical of Manfred's works, but he says he did not set out to write historical novels. He did not want to let the facts spoil the story. "If I feel like it I'll re-arrange the facts to make the book more truthful," he told a group at the University of Minnesota.[30] An example of what he means can be seen in his handling of the facts of the great Sioux uprising of 1862 out of which *Scarlet Plume* was written. The letters he read from Colonel Sibley provided the germ for Judith in that novel, but they had been edited, and some "raw stuff" had been left out. There were hints that the German women had done something horrible as the Indians marched from New Ulm to Mankato, because Sibley had sent them back to New Ulm unprotected. Manfred imagined that, driven to fury by the atrocities the Indians had been accused of committing, they had emasculated some of the braves with butcher knives. A few years later, his imagination was proven accurate when a letter was found from a German woman who had lived in New Ulm at the time.[31]

Manfred says that in the Buckskin Man Tales he is painting a "long hallway of written murals" in an attempt to create a fictional, though historically accurate, country, much as Faulkner did with his Yoknapatawpha County.[32]

In order to be historically accurate, Manfred makes massive reading lists for each novel and conducts many interviews with knowledgeable people. For example, he read more than one hundred books in preparation of writing *Lord Grizzly*, and for *Conquering Horse*, he interviewed a full-blooded Indian woman in her eighties, whose grandmother had told her of the prewhite days.

Before writing *Riders of Judgment,* he talked at length with descendants of the warring factions in the Johnson range wars.

Even though solidly based on history, the Buckskin Man Tales are more than "historical novels" or "Westerns." The books can be seen as a working out of universal themes in a Western setting. John Milton has said that Manfred is "engaged in the revealing of the characters and the destiny of man in Western America, and, by extension, in the Western world."[33] In fact, a single dominant universal theme could be assigned to each tale, such as "initiation" in *Conquering Horse,* "guilt" in *Lord Grizzly,* "love" in *Scarlet Plume,* "greed" in *King of Spades,* and "family curse" in *Riders of Judgment.* While each book is more complex than such labels would imply, yet each is most importantly also simply a storyteller's tale.

B. *Philosophical*

Although Manfred does not fit neatly into any philosophical school, his writing has tempted students and scholars to give him labels. At least two theses have been written to show that his writing is naturalistic.[34] Others like to see his work as realistic in a certain way or as influenced by existentialism. Elements of both the classical and the romantic can be found. Why Manfred's writing is difficult to categorize may be seen from the following summary of the points of view.

According to the theories of the literary naturalists, who took their cue from the revolution in thought produced by modern science, everything real exists in nature, and nature's secrets can be found through scientific inquiry. Man is seen as an animal in the natural world, responding to hereditary and environmental forces over which he has no control. Mechanistic determinism derived from Newton and biological determinism derived from Darwin give naturalism a pessimistic tone.[35]

In Manfred's works, there are many images of man as animal. Hugh Glass in *Lord Grizzly* is an outstanding example, for he wraps himself in a bear skin and survives as an animal might; No Name in *Conquering Horse* learns how to be husband and father by watching the stallion Dancing Sun; Juhl in *Milk of Wolves* returns to the deep woods and survives by imitating animal ways; Whitebone in *Scarlet Plume* sees the white man as an animal because he has his face and chest covered with hair, and Scarlet Plume tells Judith that the Yanktons are cousins to the deer.

Evidence that man is determined by heredity and environment

can be found in several books. In *Riders of Judgment*, the hereditary family curse, the "wild streak," is seen to dominate the action through Gramp Hammett's influence; in *King of Spades*, the King family's origins in England and the animal drives of sex and jealousy seem to make Ransom a victim of blind chance; in much the same way Jack Nagel and Liz in *Morning Red*, Garrett in *The Man Who Looked Like The Prince of Wales*, Brandt in *Eden Prairie*, and Elof in *The Chokecherry Tree* seem to have little control over the destinies heredity and environment have marked out for them. Manfred's notion that place chooses man rather than man choosing place is a naturalistic view.

Existentialism may share some pessimism with naturalism in seeing chance or meaninglessness in the outer world, but it denies that man is helpless. He is totally free to act upon that world and is therefore, according to the existentialist, responsible for his own destiny. This, of course, causes him a certain amount of anxiety. On the other hand, he is not trapped. He can alter society and the human condition, but only by making such alterations within himself and by making personal choices.[36] Reason, though, is not enough. Improvement can come only by uniting the irrational and rational parts of the psyche.

It is in his recognition of the irrational aspects of the psyche that Manfred comes closest to the existential view. As discussed earlier in this chapter, his emphasis on mysticism in the Buckskin Man Tales, his identification with the "Old Lizard" or the primordial, and his reliance upon dreams indicate an effort on his part to represent the whole man. The pure naturalist, of course, would deny the validity of a mystical experience.

In *Boy Almighty* there is a blend of naturalistic and existential elements. On one hand, Eric Frey with his tuberculosis seems to be the victim of indifferent environmental and hereditary forces symbolized in "The Whipper," but in the end Eric survives through the "inner" awareness of his own integrity as given to him through the good influence of Dr. Abraham and Dr. Fawkes. In commenting on his own experience with tuberculosis, Manfred said, "It [the universe] was probably just indifferent to us all. Whatever we had we made ourselves, and we make the Whipper in our own image" (92). Man, then, can alter his world.

One way to confront meaninglessness is to accept it and be happy. Albert Camus, in his essay on the myth of Sisyphus, concludes that Sisyphus must be happy as he rolls his rock forever. Elof

Lofblom comes to that same kind of acceptance in *The Choke-cherry Tree* as he settles down to the rolling of his particular rock, pumping gas on Chokecherry Corner.

Just as the elements of naturalism and existentialism are blended in Manfred's work, so too are elements of classicism and romanticism. In a book like *Conquering Horse*, there is an imitation of the classical epic form, with attention paid to restraint, restricted scope, clarity, simplicity, and balance. On the other hand, the tradition of the "romance" can be found in such works as *Morning Red* and *Milk of Wolves*, where the structure is less concise, incidents are somewhat remote from ordinary life, and there are deliberate digressions. From the standpoint of literary philosophy, Manfred is a romanticist in his placing the individual at the center of art, in the high premium he puts on creative imagination, and in his belief that intuitive perceptions tend to speak a nobler truth than that of fact or logic.

In seeking the ideal by transcending the actual, Manfred would seem not to be a realist or a naturalist. However, especially in his best autobiographical novels, such as *Green Earth*, he writes in a strict realistic mode, which would satisfy Henry James. In "The Art of Fiction," James wrote: "A novel is in its broadest definition a personal, a direct impression of life: that, to begin with, constitutes its value, which is greater or less according to the intensity of the impression. But there will be no intensity at all, and therefore no value, unless there is freedom to feel and say."[37]

By insisting upon his freedom to "feel and say," Manfred has brought criticism upon his work for being too "realistic," as in the brutal massacre scenes of *Scarlet Plume*, the sexual scenes of *The Man Who Looked Like the Prince of Wales* and *Eden Prairie*, or the "barnyard" humor in *Green Earth*. His realism, then, has not been the "gentle realism" of William Dean Howells, who would have novelists write so as not to offend innocent young girls. Manfred does not write for his Aunt Kathryn, who would not read his books, but he does follow the notion expressed by Howells in "Criticism and Fiction" that the true realist finds "in life nothing insignificant; all tells for destiny and character; nothing that God has made is contemptible."[38] Henry James puts it this way: "the province of art is all life, all feeling, all observation, all vision . . . all experience."[39]

This all-inclusiveness is evident to one who reads all of Manfred's novels, for he is trying to show us "how we are" in our totality. But he can be seen as a realist in a peculiarly "Western American" sense, as well, a sense Max Westbrook calls "Western realism" or "sacralist." Westbrook points out that where writers from the eastern half of the United States emphasize good will and consciousness in the quest for realism, the writers from the American West measure whether events are real or unreal according to whether or not they show the inner self in contact with the universal. Such "sacralist" writers thus recognize, according to Westbrook, both the practical and the spiritual which are so paradoxically a part of the American tradition. Simply put, "the sacred man does not find a *symbol* of God; he finds God."[40]

In the tradition of "sacrality," Westbrook names such diverse writers as Wallace Stevens and Michael Straight, Walt Whitman and Tom Lea, Thomas Wolfe and Frank Waters, John Steinbeck and Robert Bly, Walter Van Tilburg Clark and Lawrence Ferlinghetti, Frederick Manfred and D. H. Lawrence, Vardis Fisher and James Baldwin. That Manfred is listed in the tradition is a recognition that his work deals with at least three themes of sacrality: the commitment to cyclical rather than linear time, the recognition of the continuity of life, and the search for the original source. The search for that source has brought Manfred back to Siouxland, where he lets the tone of the place reverberate through his tales, where he can feel in his bones, as Hugh Glass did, the primal energy, the "connection between the irrational variety of himself and the irrational variety of the universe . . . to achieve a unity of the practical world with the world of spirit."[41]

CHAPTER 6

Postscript

EVEN though Frederick Manfred is in his sixties at this
writing, he talks as though he were just beginning to tap the resources of Siouxland. Another manuscript was completed in 1978.
Therefore, this concluding note is not intended to be a "final"
assessment of the author, but rather a marker along the road of his
career. Whether that road has been up or down, Manfred through it
all has remained optimistic and has continued his daily routine of
writing, a professional novelist through and through. He must be
judged on the accumulated body of his work.

The temptation is to look at that work, note his careful tie to the
Siouxland region, and see in Manfred the midwest's William
Faulkner. Though both authors deal with regional themes related to
growth and decay of the society around them, and though each has
gone his own way with language, the comparison is not very helpful. Manfred's novels do not fit into neat categories. One might as
well see in him a Thomas Wolfe when reading *Green Earth* or
Wanderlust, a John Steinbeck in *The Golden Bowl*, a Frank Waters
or a Vardis Fisher in the Buckskin Man Tales, a Willa Cather in
This is the Year or *Eden Prairie*, an Erskine Caldwell in *The Man
Who Looked Like the Prince of Wales*. Ultimately, one must look at
the particular books of the author.

Easily the most popular of Manfred's books have been the Buckskin Man Tales, with *Lord Grizzly* heading the list. Because they
have been easily available in paperback, they have been used frequently in high school and college literature classes. Students like
them. *Lord Grizzly* is most dense with symbolic meaning, *Conquering Horse* is most revealing of Indian ways, and *Scarlet Plume* is
most dramatic in its realistic treatment of the great Sioux uprising.
Each is "best" in its own way, and all three are better than the
other tales. Nevertheless, *Riders of Judgment* is a strong cowboy
story, and *The Manly-Hearted Woman* in time may be seen as

equal to *Conquering Horse*. *King of Spades* is the weakest tale in the group, in spite of some beautifully rendered scenes with Erden. Over all, though, its focus is too much divided between the historical account of the Black Hills gold rush and an elaborate retelling of the Oedipus myth.

Among the novels, *The Golden Bowl* and *This is the Year* are of highest quality, yet they have opposing virtues. That is, *The Golden Bowl* has an intense gemlike quality, while *This is the Year* achieves its power through a deliberate build up of details about farm life. *Eden Prairie* is next in importance, but it does not have the universal appeal of the other two novels. Its characters seem contrived to fit the theme of the innocent versus the vulgar on the prairie. *The Chokecherry Tree* is fun to read, but the authorial introductions to chapters cannot give the book the significance intended, for it remains a series of minor adventures at a country crossroads, and the same could be said for *The Man Who Looked Like the Prince of Wales*.

Of the rumes, *Green Earth* is easily the best work. The author had ample time to "ruminate" over his material and to bring forth a book in loving honesty. *Wanderlust*, even in the newer version, is too self-conscious in its examination of the author's life; and *Boy Almighty*, while a powerful personal statement, still has the immaturity of a second novel when compared to the more profound *Green Earth*.

The most difficult books to assess are *Morning Red* and *Milk of Wolves*. They have been the least attractive to publishers and critics. Because they are not easily available, they have been given a rather full summarization and discussion in previous pages. Of the two, *Milk of Wolves* has the better chance of republication and revival. It is less didactic than *Morning Red* and more subtle in its handling of ideas. Yet it shares with *Morning Red* the disturbing characteristic of startling readers with bizarre incidents, exaggerated characterizations, and lengthy dissertations. Faced with these elements, a reader is tempted to say, "You've got to be kidding." Even so, one has to be glad that Manfred wrote them, not only because they contain many ideas important to the author, but also because they provide a unique reading experience, offering a strong narrative pull and plenty of surprises.

The best evaluation of Manfred's work to date is the foreword that Wallace Stegner wrote for *Conversations with Frederick Manfred*. Stegner sees Manfred in one way as hobbled by his Siouxland region, as being a shade too provincial and unable to stand outside the place, but on the other hand as being able to expand easily and powerfully from history and reality to myth. Thus, Stegner thinks Manfred writes better about the authentic heroes of the Buckskin Man Tales than he does about the obscure farm boys he grew up among.[1]

While Stegner is right in pointing to the tales as Manfred at his best, it is also true that some of his best writing appears in the farm novels, where he tells "how it was" in those Siouxland days: stacking hay, husking corn, castrating pigs, playing ball, dating the girls. As Arthur Miller speaks for the Willy Lomans, so Fred Manfred speaks for the Elof Lofbloms. "Attention must be paid," Willy's wife says. "He is human too." Manfred is a "voice" for his Siouxland people, for all the people, including the Indians who first inhabited the place. Giving readers an authentic interpretation of Indian life may well be Manfred's most significant contribution.

Readers of Manfred in the 1970s may find his celebration of the human male to be "old fashioned" in view of the current celebration of the human female; on the other hand, readers will find Manfred's call for a transformation in human consciousness to be both prophetic and optimistic about the future.

It is ironic that the fascination with words and language that enables Manfred to invent an appropriate way of speaking for Indians would also in other books lead him into trouble with the critics. Stegner says that he "wrenches and shoves at his verbs," and that his "impatience with linguistic patterns leads him into frequent neologisms, whose effect on dramatic illusion is that of a splinter on a nylon stocking"[2]. Many of Manfred's coinages are effective, but others shout for attention and distract the reader. The same is true for his use of extravagant names or nicknames, especially in *Riders of Judgment* and in the three books of the early trilogy.

On the other hand, Manfred has a good ear for colloquial speech patterns and is a master storyteller. His style has been influenced by daily reading of the Bible in his youth and by a love for Chaucer, whose language reminds him of the Frisian. He is an avid reader of the Greek classics and of Shakespeare, his favorite play being *Hamlet*. On his hitchhiking trips he always carried the Bible, Shakespeare, and Whitman—a favorite American poet. In his books, he quotes at some length from such writers as Hemingway, Twain, Veblen, Emerson, Poe, and Longfellow. Of the other American writers, he finds Faulkner most rewarding.[3] He did not know

Faulkner personally, but he did have a close friendship and cor-
respondence with Vardis Fisher and Frank Waters.

Manfred shares with Vardis Fisher a loving concern for "place,"
along with a pessimism about what has happened and is happening
to the environment as a result of the "Jehovah" complex that has
driven the westward movement. As Frank Waters has documented
the effects of that movement on the native cultures of the American
Southwest, Manfred has recorded the white encroachment on Plains
cultures.

An early apocalyptic vision of danger ahead is given in O. E.
Rolvaag's *Giants in the Earth,* a book Manfred knew as a youth.
Where Per Hansa in that book is often seen as a pioneer hero opening up the endless prairies, his optimism is challenged by his wife,
Beret, who, Cassandralike, has a dark vision of what is to come. She
saw that the heroic action of taming the land could turn it into
something less than Eden. As we now know, she was right. The
prairies were not endless, the void has become full, and there has
been a second "fall."

In *This is the Year,* Manfred shows us that "fall" in Pier Frixen,
who seems to be descended from Per Hansa. For that matter, Manfred's Bonnie, Willa Cather's Black Hawk, and Sinclair Lewis's
Gopher Prairie all continue to reveal the truth of Beret's vision by
showing the tragedy of Americanization—the cost in lives, culture,
heritage, even in loss of soul. But the vision is not all that dark,
either. Cather's Alexandra in *O Pioneers!* has a positive relationship
with the land, is in love with "the spirit of the Great Divide," just as
Manfred's Alfred and Ada in *Green Earth* lovingly bring several
rented farms to life and are ennobled in the process.

It is in showing this ennobling process, this balancing of good and
bad, innocent and vulgar, that Manfred softens his pessimism with
optimism and makes his most significant contribution to American
literature. That contribution is represented powerfully in each of
the forms Manfred has chosen for his art—particularly in the rume
Green Earth, the tale *Scarlet Plume,* and the novel *Eden Prairie.*
With more than twenty books to his credit interpreting mid-
America, Frederick Manfred deserves recognition as a major American novelist.

But Manfred is not simply an American novelist. He is a majestic
personality, somewhat like one of his favorite writers, Charles
Doughty, who wrote *Dawn in Britain* and *Travels in Arabia Deser-
ta.* Manfred first read Doughty in 1944, and since then he has

quoted him more than a dozen times in his books. He may have sensed a kindred spirit in the English writer, who also was self-secure, a disciple of Chaucer, dedicated to improvement of his native tongue, and drawn by a feeling for the primitive.[4]

G. B. Shaw wrote the following about Charles Doughty in *Back to Methuselah:* "There must have been something majestic or gigantic about the man that made him classic in himself. . . . Englishmen who met him have described him to me as a mountain of a man."[5] Wallace Stegner writes of Manfred: "He is not a writer in the usual sense. He is a natural force, related to hurricanes, deluges, volcanic eruptions, and the ponderous formation of continents."[6]

Notes and References

Chapter One

1. *Conversations With Frederick Manfred,* moderated by John R. Milton (Salt Lake City, 1974), p. 2. Much of the information in this chapter has been gathered from the above reference, hereafter abbreviated to *Conversations,* and from interviews with Frederick Manfred. To simplify reading, references to *Conversations* will be given within the body, preceded by the letter "C." References to other Manfred books will be given in the body by number alone. Editions referred to are the ones cited in the bibliography.

2. Dan Hager, "The Frisians Among Us," *Grand Rapids Press,* 19 January 1975, p. 24.

3. Both "Feike" and "Feikema" were mispronounced from the beginning, and Manfred feared the sales of his books were being hurt. Beginning with *Lord Grizzly,* a book which marked a turning point in his career, the novelist added Manfred to his legal name of Frederick Feikema. Through research he had found that Feikema anglicized meant Fredman, or Manfred, an Anglo-Saxon name he liked. He found, too, that the translation of Feike to Frank was wrong and that Fred or Frederick was the authentic Frisian translation. By chance his maternal grandfather's name coincided with the true translation of the Frisian "Feike."

4. Hager, p. 23.

5. "Sinclair Lewis' Funeral and In Memoriam Address," *South Dakota Review,* 7 (Winter 1969 - 70) 55.

6. *Wanderlust* (Denver, 1962), p. 156.

7. Ibid., p. 220.

8. Interview, June 13, 1975.

9. Ibid.

10. "Sinclair Lewis: A Portrait," *The American Scholar,* 23 (Spring 1954), 162 - 84.

11. "Sinclair Lewis' Funeral," p. 58.

12. Ibid., p. 58.

13. "Siouxland" is the term Manfred coined for his home region, that prairie land which centers on the point where Iowa, Minnesota, and South Dakota meet. He says that the concept of Siouxland came to him as he was writing *This is the Year,* his third novel. He has since held to his determination that in every book there would be someone who would live in Siouxland.

Chapter Two

1. Lecture at Southwest State University, Marshall, Minnesota, 27 April 1978.

2. In the postscript to *Giant,* Manfred explains that his first title for the book was *The Golden Bowl Be Broken.* "Would that I had kept it!" he writes. He says the words have no reference to the Henry James novel of the same title.

3. *The Golden Bowl* (Saint Paul, 1944), p. 209. Following references to this work will be given in the text.

4. "West of the Mississippi: An Interview with Frederick Manfred," *Critique,* 2 (Winter 1959) 35 - 36.

5. Peter P. De Boer, "Frederick Manfred: The Developing Art of the Novelist," Masters Thesis, University of Iowa, 1961, p. 15.

6. "West of the Mississippi," p. 46.

7. *This is the Year* (Garden City, 1947), pp. 465 - 66. Following references to this work will be given in the text.

8. "West of the Mississippi," p. 38.

9. De Boer, p. 45.

10. Roy W. Meyer, *The Middle Western Farm Novel* (Lincoln, University of Nebraska, 1965), p. 193.

11. *The Chokecherry Tree* (New York, 1948), p. 121. Following references to this work will be given in the text.

12. Albert Camus, *The Myth of Sisyphus and Other Essays* (New York, 1959), p. 91.

13. Albert C. Baugh, Tucker Brooke, George Sherburn, and Samuel C. Chew, *A Literary History of England* (New York, 1948), p. 962.

14. Frank Waters, *The Man Who Killed the Deer* (Denver, 1942), p. 296.

15. Ibid., p. 302.

16. De Boer, pp. 61 - 64.

17. Later published as *The Secret Place* by Pocketbooks in 1967.

18. *The Man Who Looked Like the Prince of Wales* (New York, 1965), p. 13. Following references to this work will be given in the text.

19. Lecture at Southwest State University, Marshall, Minnesota, 26 April 1978.

20. *Eden Prairie* (New York, 1968) p. 281. Following references to this work will be given in the text.

21. Plato, *Great Dialogues of Plato* trans. W. H. D. Rouse, ed. Eric H. Warmington (New York, 1956), p. 86.

Chapter Three

1. Russell Roth, "The Inception of a Saga: Frederick Manfred's 'Buckskin Man,'" *South Dakota Review,* 7, no. 4 (Winter 1969 - 1970), 88.

2. Ibid., p. 89.

3. Jacque Suzanne Funderburk Pruett, "A Critical Analysis of Lord Grizzly," Masters Thesis, Colorado State University, 1968, p. 156.

4. Ibid., p. 153.

5. Mick McAllister, "We sons of Jacob: The Procession to Apocalypse in the Buckskin Man Tales" (paper presented to the Western Literature Association, Sioux Falls, S. D., October 1977).

6. James C. Austin, "Legend, Myth and Symbol in Frederick Manfred's *Lord Grizzly, Critique,* 6 (Winter 1963 - 1964), 123.

7. Russell Roth, "Is Manfred the Midwest's Faulkner?" *Minneapolis Sunday Tribune,* 1 August 1954, p. 1.

8. Notebook on *Lord Grizzly,* University of Minnesota Archives, Minneapolis, Minnesota.

9. J. E. Cirlot, *A Dictionary of Symbols,* trans. Jack Sage (New York, 1962), p. 222.

10. Ibid., pp. 224 - 25.

11. John R. Milton, "Lord Grizzly: Rhythm, Form and Meaning in the Western Novel," *Western American Literature,* 1 (Spring 1966), pp. 6 - 14.

12. Pruett, p. 58. Jacque Pruett's thesis on Manfred's *Lord Grizzly* is the most thorough study of the novel to date, a fully documented and perceptive analysis which was most helpful in the preparation of this section.

13. Ibid., p. 58.

14. *Lord Grizzly* (New York, 1954), p. 14. **Following references to this work will be given in the text.**

15. **Edgeley W. Todd, "James Hall and the Hugh Glass Legend,"** *American Studies Quarterly,* (December 1953), pp. 362 - 70.

16. Pruett, p. 63.

17. Ibid., p. 59.

18. John R. Milton, "Voice from Siouxland: Frederick Feikema Manfred," *College English,* 19 (December 1957), 104 - 11.

19. Austin, pp. 126 - 28.

20. Cirlot, pp. 224 - 25.

21. Sir James Frazer, *The New Golden Bough,* ed. Theodore H. Gastner (New York, 1959), pp. 505 - 18.

22. Austin, pp. 126 - 28.

23. Pruett, p. 109.

24. Austin, pp. 122 - 30.

25. D. H. Lawrence, *Studies in Classic American Literature* (New York, 1964), p. 6.

26. Pruett, p. 108.

27. John G. Neihardt, *Black Elk Speaks* (New York, 1972), pp. 159 - 60.

28. Sophocles, *Antigone,* in *Seven Famous Greek Plays,* eds. Whitney J. Oates and Eugene O'Neill, Jr. (New York, 1950), p. 212.

29. Nathaniel Hawthorne, "Roger Malvin's Burial," in *The Complete Novels and Selected Tales of Hawthorne,* ed. Norman Pearson (New York, 1937), p. 1132.

30. Quoted by John K. Sherman in the *Minneapolis Star*, 26 September 1954.

31. McAllister.

32. Papers for *Riders of Judgment*, University of Minnesota Archives, Minneapolis, Minnesota.

33. Ibid.

34. *Riders of Judgment* (New York, 1957), p. 287. Following references to this work will be given in the text.

35. De Boer, p. 138.

36. Ibid., p. 156.

37. Edith Hamilton, *Mythology* (New York, 1942), pp. 236 - 48.

38. Ibid., p. 248.

39. De Boer, p. 150.

40. Joseph M. Flora, *Frederick Manfred* (Boise, 1947), pp. 42 - 43.

41. D. E. Wylder, "Manfred's Indian Novel," *South Dakota Review*, 7, no. 4 (Winter 1969 - 70) pp. 100 - 10.

42. William Thrall and Addison Hibbard, *A Handbook to Literature*, rev. C. Hugh Holman (New York, 1960), pp. 174 - 75.

43. *Conquering Horse* (New York, 1959), p. 151. Following references to this work will be given in the text.

44. Walt Whitman, *Leaves of Grass* (New York, 1959), p. 151.

45. Manuscript on file at the *Mankato Free Press*, Mankato, Minnesota.

46. Notebook on *Scarlet Plume*, University of Minnesota Archives, Minneapolis, Minnesota.

47. *Scarlet Plume* (New York, 1964), p. 26. Following references to this work will be given in the text.

48. Notes for *Scarlet Plume*, University of Minnesota Archives, Minneapolis, Minnesota.

49. Archives copy of *Scarlet Plume*, University of Minnesota Archives, Minneapolis, Minnesota.

50. *King of Spades* (New York, 1966), p. 6. Following references to this work will be given in the text.

51. Russell Roth, review of *King of Spades*, *Western American Literature*, 1, no. 4 (Winter 1967) 302 - 04.

52. Roth, "The Inception of a Saga," p. 89.

53. Lawrence, p. 6.

54. Herbert Krause, letter in Archives, University of Minnesota, Minneapolis, Minnesota.

55. *The Manly-Hearted Woman* (New York, 1975), p. 75. Following references to this work will be given in the text.

56. Walt Whitman, *Leaves of Grass and Selected Prose*, ed. John Kouwenhoven (New York, 1950), p. 38.

57. Frazer, p. 643.

58. Cirlot, p. 223.

59. Whitman, p. 28.

60. Delbert Wylder, "Frederick Manfred and Colin Stuart," (paper presented to the Western Literature Association, Sioux Falls, S. D., October, 1977).

Chapter Four

1. Frederick Manfred, postscript to *Giant* (New York, 1951), p. 403.
2. Ibid., p. 408.
3. Frederick Manfred, *Boy Almighty* (Saint Paul, 1945), p. 20. Following references to this work will be given in the text.
4. Alan Watts, *The Book* (New York, 1972), p. 132.
5. Van Wyck Brooks, letter to Manfred, 4 March 1946, in *Boy Almighty* file, University of Minnesota archives, Minneapolis, Minnesota.
6. Peter Oppewall, "Manfred and Calvin College," in *Where the West Begins*, Arthur R. Huseboe and William Geyer, eds., (Sioux Falls, 1978), p. 97.
7. Larry A. Michael, "Literary Allusions in the Fiction of Frederick Manfred," Thesis, University of South Dakota, 1965, p. 37.
8. Manfred, *Giant*, p. 424.
9. Ibid., p. 425.
10. Ibid., p. 419.
11. Ibid., p. 425.
12. Frederick Manfred, *Winter Count* (Minneapolis, 1966), p. 14.
13. Frederick Manfred, unpublished poem.
14. Frederick Manfred, *Morning Red* (Denver, 1956), p. 562. Following references to this work will be given in the text.
15. De Boer, p. 114.
16. Ibid., p. 104.
17. Unidentified clipping in file on *Morning Red*, University of Minnesota archives, Minneapolis, Minnesota.
18. Archives copy of *Morning Red*, University of Minnesota archives, Minneapolis, Minnesota.
19. Frederick Manfred, *Milk of Wolves* (Boston, 1976), p. 249. Following references to this work will be given in the text.
20. Lawrence, p. 137.
21. Harry T. Moore, *D. H. Lawrence: His Life and Works*, rev. ed. (New York, 1964), p. 217.
22. Ibid., p. 272.
23. Whitman, p. 61.
24. Ibid., p. 50.
25. John Fowles, *The Aristos* (New York, 1970), p. 61.
26. Colin Wilson, *The Outsider* (New York, 1967), p. 13 - 15.
27. Frederick Manfred, *Arrow of Love* (Denver, 1961), p. 44. Following references to this work will be given in the text.
28. Mark Vinz, ed. "Milton, Manfred, and McGrath: A Conversation on

Literature and Place," *Dacotah Territory*, 8/9 (Fall-Winter 1974 - 1975), p. 26.

29. Whitman, p. 104.

30. Ibid., p. 105.

31. Frederick Manfred, *Apples of Paradise* (New York, 1968), p. 11. Following references to this work will be given in the text.

32. Frederick Manfred, *Winter Count* (Minneapolis, 1966), p. 37. Following references to this work will be given in the text.

Chapter Five

1. Max Westbrook, "The Practical Spirit: Sacrality and the American West," *Western Writing* ed. Gerald W. Haslam (Albuquerque, 1974), p. 12.

2. Lawrence, p. 6.

3. Ibid., p. 7.

4. "Writing in the West," cassette tape (Deland, Florida, 1974).

5. Vinz, p. 23.

6. "Writing in the West."

7. Donald Bebeau, "A Search for Voice, A Sense of Place in The Golden Bowl," *South Dakota Review*, 7, no. 4 (Winter 1969 - 1970) 79 - 87.

8. "West of the Mississippi," p. 53.

9. Vinz, p. 23.

10. John Milton, "Interview with Frederick Manfred," *South Dakota Review*, 7, no. 4 (Winter 1969 - 1970) 114.

11. Ibid., p. 115 - 116.

12. Ibid., pp. 110 - 113.

13. Whitman, "Passage to India," p. 321.

14. Robin Wright, in a letter to the author, expressed the preceding ideas on mysticism in the Buckskin Man Tales.

15. Waters, p. 154.

16. Antone C. Zijderveld, *The Abstract Society* (Garden City, N.Y., 1971), p. 66.

17. Ibid., p. 165.

18. Ibid., p. 165.

19. Joyce Carol Oates, "A New Heaven and Earth," *Saturday Review*, 4 November 1972, p. 54.

20. Ibid., p. 19.

21. *Minneapolis Sunday Tribune*, 25 October 1964.

22. Lionel Tiger and Robin Fox, *The Imperial Animal* (New York, 1971), p. 60.

23. Ibid., p. 62.

24. Ibid., p. 63.

25. Ibid., p. 70.

26. Ibid., p. 115.

27. Ibid., p. 116 - 117.

28. Lionel Tiger, *Men in Groups* (New York, 1969), p. 199.

29. Ibid., p. 210.

30. Dave Daley, "Truth, Not Facts Is 'Historical' Novelist's Goal," *Minneapolis Star*, 4 September 1975, p. 2C.

31. Frederick Manfred, lecture at Mankato State University, 1 April 1974.

32. Daley, p. 2C.

33. John R. Milton, "Voice from Siouxland: Frederick Feikema Manfred," p. 111.

34. Gordon P. Gits, "The Buckskin Man Tales of Frederick Manfred: Realistic or Naturalistic?" Masters Thesis, Mankato State University, June 1971; and Richard P. O'Brien, "Naturalism and the Tragic View in the Writing of Frederick Manfred," Masters Thesis, Mankato State University, August 1967.

35. C. Hugh Holman, William Flint Thrall, and Addison Hibbard, *A Handbook to Literature*, rev. C. Hugh Holman (New York, 1960), pp. 337 - 38.

36. Ibid., pp. 217 - 18.

37. Henry James, "The Art of Fiction," in *The American Tradition in Literature*, vol. II, rev., eds. Bradley, Beatty, Long (New York, 1961), pp. 659, 660.

38. William Dean Howells, "Criticism and Fiction," in *American Literature* II, ed. George McMichael (New York, 1974), p. 601.

39. James, p. 667.

40. Max Westbrook, "Conservative, Liberal, and Western: Three Modes of American Realism," *South Dakota Review*, 4, no. 2 (Summer 1966), p. 12.

41. Max Westbrook, "The Practical Spirit: Sacrality and the American West," in *Western Writing*, ed. Gerald W. Haslam (Albuquerque, 1974), pp. 133 - 34.

Chapter Six

1. Wallace Stegner, preface to *Conversations with Frederick Manfred*, p. Cxii.

2. Ibid., p. Cxi.

3. Larry A. Michael, "Literary Allusions in the Fiction of Frederick Manfred," Thesis, University of South Dakota, 1965, pp. 24 - 25.

4. Baugh et al., pp. 1541 and 1592.

5. G. B. Shaw, quoted in Michael, p. 25.

6. Stegner, p. Cxi.

Selected Bibliography

PRIMARY SOURCES

1. Books

The Golden Bowl. Saint Paul: Webb Publishing Co., 1944; Vermillion, S.D.: Dakota Press, 1969, slightly rev. ed., with Introduction by John R. Milton.

Boy Almighty. Saint Paul: Webb Publishing Co., 1945.

This is the Year. Garden City, N. Y.: Doubleday, 1947.

The Chokecherry Tree. Garden City, N. Y.: Doubleday, 1948; rev. ed., Denver: Alan Swallow, 1961; Albuquerque: University of New Mexico Press, 1975, with Introduction by Delbert E. Wylder.

The Primitive. Garden City, N. Y.: Doubleday, 1949.

The Brother. Garden City, N. Y.: Doubleday, 1950.

The Giant. Garden City, N. Y.: Doubleday, 1951.

Lord Grizzly. New York: McGraw Hill, 1954; New York: Pocket Books, 1955; New York: New American Library (Signet), 1964; London: Transworld Publishers, Ltd., 1957.

Morning Red. Denver: Alan Swallow, 1956.

Riders of Judgment. New York: Random House, 1957; Toronto: McLeod, 1957; New York: Pocket Books, 1958.

Conquering Horse. New York: McDowell, Obolensky, 1959; New York: New American Library (Signet), 1965.

Arrow of Love. Denver: Alan Swallow, 1961.

Wanderlust. Denver: Alan Swallow, 1962.

Scarlet Plume. New York: Trident Press, 1964; New York: New American Library (Signet), 1973.

The Man Who Looked Like the Prince of Wales. New York: Trident Press, 1965; republished as *The Secret Place*. New York: Pocket Books, 1967.

King of Spades. New York: Trident Press, 1966; New York: New American Library (Signet), 1973.

Winter Count. Minneapolis: James D. Thueson, 1966. (Poems)

Eden Prairie. New York: Trident Press, 1968.

Apples of Paradise. New York: Trident Press, 1968. (Short Stories)

Conversations with Frederick Manfred. Moderated by John R. Milton. With an introduction by Wallace Stegner. Salt Lake City: The University of Utah Press, 1974.

The Manly-Hearted Woman. New York: Crown, 1976; New York: New American Library (Signet), 1977.

Milk of Wolves. Boston: Avenue Victor Hugo, 1976.

Green Earth. New York: Crown, 1977.

172

2. Uncollected Fiction in Periodicals

"Child Delinquent." *Northwest Life*, 16 (March 1944), 26 - 27.

"Horse Touch." *Northwest Life*, 18 (May 1945), 18 - 20.

"Judith: A Fragment." *Plainsong*, 2 (Winter 1950), 4 - 13.

"Omen of Spring." *Minnesota Quarterly*, (Winter 1950), 4 - 13.

"The Voice of the Turtle." *South Dakota Review*, 11 (Autumn 1973), 89 - 105.

"Where the Grass Grows Greenest." *The Farmer*, 72 (June 6, 1953), 14 - 15, 32 - 33; (June 20, 1953), 10, 25.

3. Essays and Reviews

"Author Nicks Self on Edge of Own Wit." *Chicago Sun Times*, March 8, 1950, Section II, p. 6.

"Backgrounds for Western Writing." *The Denver Westerner's Monthly Roundup*, 17 (August 1961), 4 - 11.

"Children of the Motherland." *The Saturday Review*, 43 (June 4, 1960), 31.

"Derleth on Schorer and Staying at Home." *Sinclair Lewis Newsletter*, 3 (1971), 21.

"The Evolution of a Name." *Names*, 2 (1954), 106 - 108.

"Frederick Manfred Talks about Sinclair Lewis." *Sinclair Lewis Newsletter*, 1 (Spring 1970), 1 - 5.

"Flesh Compass." *The New York Times Book Review*, January 12, 1975.

"Hareb's Temptation." *The New York Times Book Review*, December 8, 1957, p. 50.

"In Memoriam Address (On the Occasion of the Burial of Sinclair Lewis' Ashes in Sauk Centre, Minnesota, January 28, 1951)." *The Minneapolis Labor Review*, 44 (February 15, 1951), 3.

"Letters to the Journal." *The Reformed Journal*, 13 (May - June 1963), 24.

"Little Innovation?" Letter to *The Saturday Review*, March 12, 1949, pp. 19 - 20.

"Manfred Talks About Characters." *The Minneapolis Tribune* (Open Forum Section), December 16, 1956, p. 3.

"Mountain Man." Review of Vardis Fisher's *Mountain Man*. *Western American Literature*, 1 (Spring 1966), 59.

"Report from Minnesota," *New Republic*, 109 (October 11, 1943), 480 - 81.

"Sinclair Lewis: A Portrait." *The American Scholar*, 23 (Spring 1954), 162 - 84.

"Sinclair Lewis' Funeral, and In Memoriam Address." *South Dakota Review*, 7 (Winter 1969 - 70), 54 - 78.

"Some Notes on Sinclair Lewis' Funeral." *The Minnesota Review*, 3 (Fall 1962), 87 - 90.

"Speaking of Books." *The New York Times Book Review*, February 12, 1956, p. 2.

"Wanted: More Ornery Cusses." *Chicago Sunday Tribune Book Review*,
    December 4, 1955, p. 24.
"The Western Novel—A Symposium: Frederick Manfred." *South Dakota
    Review*, 2 (Autumn 1964), 7 - 9.
"Writing in the West." Cassette tape. Deland, Florida: Everett / Edwards,
    Inc., 1974.

SECONDARY SOURCES

1. Books and Articles

AUSTIN, JAMES C. "Legend, Myth and Symbol in Frederick Manfred's *Lord
    Grizzly*. *Critique*, 6 (Winter 1963 - 1964), 122 - 30. Identifies Hugh
    Glass as father of the New American, *Lord Grizzly* as beginning of a
    new era in the new West.

BEBEAU, DONALD. "A Search for Voice, A Sense of Place in *The Golden
    Bowl*." *South Dakota Review*, 7, no. 4 (1969 - 1970), 79 - 87. Explains
    how Manfred's first novel touches the universal through a particular
    place and gives its author a "voice."

DALEY, DAVE. "Truth, Not Facts, Is 'Historical' Novelist's Goal."
    Minneapolis Star, 4 September 1975, p. 2C. Manfred disclaims label as
    historical novelist.

FLORA, JOSEPH M. *Frederick Manfred*. Boise: Boise State University, 1974.
    A brief but usable survey of Manfred's work.

KELLOGG, GEORGE. *Frederick Manfred: A Bibliography*. Denver: Alan
    Swallow, 1965. Lists works by and about Manfred through 1965.

MEYER, ROY W. *The Middle Western Farm Novel*. Lincoln: University of
    Nebraska Press, 1965. An important survey of the farm fiction genre,
    including comment on *This is the Year*.

MILTON, JOHN R. "Frederick Feikema Manfred." *Western Review* 22
    (Spring 1958) 181 - 96. Explains Manfred's main theme as the "long
    view" of man.

———. "Interview with Frederick Manfred." *South Dakota Review*, 7, no. 4
    (Winter 1969 - 1970), 110 - 31. Manfred talks of dreams, Indians, the
    dust bowl, the Old Lizard, and father figures.

———."Lord Grizzly: Rhythm, Form and Meaning in the Western Novel."
    Western American Literature, 1 (Spring 1966), 6 - 14. Shows mystic
    fusion of man and land, animal and spirit, rational and irrational in
    Lord Grizzly as example of mature Western novel.

———. "Voice from Siouxland; Frederick Feikema Manfred." *College
    English*, 19 (December 1957), 104 - 11. Perceptive analysis of Man-
    fred's first eight novels.

ROTH, RUSSELL. "The Inception of a Saga: Frederick Manfred's 'Buckskin
    Man'." *South Dakota Review*, 7, no. 4 (Winter 1969 - 70), 87 - 100.
    Shows how the Buckskin Man Tales connect back to Cooper and ahead
    to Manfred's farm novels.

——. "Is Manfred the Midwest's Faulkner." *Minneapolis Sunday Tribune*, 1 August 1954, pp. 1 - 6. Makes a case for Manfred as a midwestern writer of stature.

SWALLOW, ALAN. "The Mavericks." *Critique*, 2 (Winter 1959), 88 - 92. A personal tribute to Manfred from a publisher.

TIGER, LIONEL. *Men in Groups*. New York: Random House, 1969. Explores the phenomenon of male groups with a view to seeing "what we are" so that we can change for the better through a changed ideal of manhood, of corporate structure, and of political acumen.

TIGER, LIONEL, and ROBIN FOX. *The Imperial Animal.* New York: Holt, Rinehart, Winston, 1971. An important contribution to the literature of the developing field of sociobiology; discusses the evolution of human behavior.

WATERS, FRANK. *The Man Who Killed the Deer*. Denver: Alan Swallow, 1942. An important contribution to the understanding of Indian culture and belief.

——. "West of the Mississippi: An Interview with Frederick Manfred." *Critique*, 2 (Winter 1959), pp. 35 - 36.

WESTBROOK, MAX. "The Practical Spirit: Sacrality and the American West." *Western Writing* ed. Gerald W. Haslam. Albuquerque: University of New Mexico Press, 1974. Defines the themes of "sacrality" as committment to cyclical time, recognition of continuity of life, and search for the original source.

——. "Conservative, Liberal, and Western: Three Modes of American Realism." *South Dakota Review*, 4, no. 2 (Summer 1966), 3 - 19. Shows how the Western realist's belief that the inner self is the contact with the universal contrasts with notions of the Conservative and Liberal realists.

WILLIAMS, JOHN. "The 'Western': Definition of a Myth." *The Nation*, 18 November 1961, pp. 401-405. Explains why there is no Faulkner or Melville of the West.

VINZ, MARK. "Milton, Manfred, and McGrath: A Conversation on Literature and Place." *Dacotah Territory*, 8/9 (Fall - Winter 1974 - 1975), 19 - 26. Manfred talks about spirit of place.

WYLDER, D. E. "Manfred's Indian Novel." *South Dakota Review*, 7, no. 4 (Winter 1969 - 70), 100 - 10. Shows how *Conquering Horse* is more epic than naturalistic.

ZIJDERVELD, ANTON. *The Abstract Society*. Garden City, N.Y.: Doubleday (Anchor), 1971. Argues against the rational trend toward more and more bureaucracy and for "intellectual aestheticism."

2. Dissertations and Theses

BOSVELD, BERNICE. "A Study of the Depression Years Through the Fiction of Frederick F. Manfred." Thesis, University of Wyoming, 1971.

DE BOER, PETER POUSMA. "Frederick Manfred: The Developing Art of the

Novelist." Masters thesis, University of Iowa, 1961. Especially critical of *Morning Red* and *Riders of Judgment*.

GITS, GORDON P. "The Buckskin Man Tales of Frederick Manfred: Realistic or Naturalistic?" Masters thesis, Mankato State University, 1971. Defends position that Buckskin Man Tales are naturalistic.

HILMOE, JOAN. "Themes of Isolation and Relationship in Selected Novels of Frederick Manfred." Thesis, South Dakota State University, 1969. Covers *Conquering Horse, Lord Grizzly, This is the Year, The Secret Place,* and *Morning Red.*

MICHAEL, LARRY A. "Literary Allusions in the Fiction of Frederick Manfred." Thesis, University of South Dakota, 1965. Identifies authors and books important to Manfred.

O'BRIEN, RICHARD P. "Naturalism and the Tragic View in the Writing of Frederick Manfred." Masters thesis, Mankato State University, 1967. Identifies naturalism in *The Golden Bowl, This is the Year, The Chokecherry Tree, Lord Grizzly,* and *Scarlet Plume.*

PEET, HOWARD. "Evolution of a Man Named Fred." Thesis, Moorhead State University, 1965. Based on interviews with Siouxland people.

PRUETT, JACQUE SUZANNE FUNDERBURK. "A Critical Analysis of *Lord Grizzly*." Masters thesis, Colorado State University, 1968. An exceptionally fine study, the definitive statement thus far on *Lord Grizzly.*

SORENSON, CHARLES SOMNER. "A Comparison of the Views of Hamsun, Rolvaag, and Feikema on Rural Society." Thesis, University of Iowa, 1955.

SPIES, GEORGE HENRY III. "John Steinbeck's *The Grapes of Wrath* and Frederick Manfred's *The Golden Bowl:* A Comparative Study." Thesis, Ball State University, 1973. Shows both books to have similarities; more humor in Steinbeck, better metaphors in Manfred.

TER MATT, CORNELIUS JOHN. "Three Novelists and a Community: A Study of American Novelists with Dutch Calvinist Origins." Dissertation, University of Michigan, 1963.

Index

177